JORGE RAMOS

A COUNTRY FOR ALL

Jorge Ramos, born in Mexico City, is an award-winning journalist and author. He is coanchor of Univision's nightly newscast, *Noticiero Univision*, and hosts *Al Punto*, the network's Sunday morning political show. Ramos also writes a weekly column distributed by the New York Times Syndicate and contributes daily analysis on Univision Radio.

He appears frequently on ABC, CBS, NBC, and CNN—among other networks—in defense of immigrant rights. He has been named one of the Most Influential Hispanics in America by *Time* magazine, and he is the recipient of eight Emmy Awards and a Maria Moors Cabot Prize for excellence in journalism. This is his tenth book.

Ramos has lived in the United States for more than twenty-five years. He has two children, Paola and Nicolás, and resides in Miami.

A COUNTRY FOR ALL

An Immigrant Manifesto

JORGE RAMOS

Translated from the Spanish by Ezra Fitz

Vintage Books
A Division of Random House, Inc.
New York

A VINTAGE BOOKS ORIGINAL, MAY 2010

Translation copyright © 2010 by Vintage Books,
a division of Random House, Inc.

All rights reserved. Published in the United States by Vintage Books, a division of
Random House, Inc., New York, and in Canada by Random House of Canada
Limited, Toronto. Originally published in Spanish in the United States by Vintage
Español, a division of Random House, Inc. Copyright © 2009 by Jorge Ramos.

Vintage and colophon are registered trademarks
of Random House, Inc.

Library of Congress Cataloging-in-Publication Data
Ramos, Jorge, 1958–
[Tierra de todos. English]
A country for all : an immigrant manifesto / Jorge Ramos ; translated
from the Spanish by Ezra Fitz.
p. cm.
ISBN: 978-0-307-47554-1
1. Hispanic Americans—Legal status, laws, etc.—United States. 2. Hispanic
Americans—Politics and government. I. Fitz, Ezra E. II. Title.
KF4757.5.L38R36 2010
342.7308'73—dc22
2009026835

www.vintagebooks.com

Printed in the United States of America
10 9 8 7 6 5 4 3 2 1

For all undocumented immigrants:
so you may have a voice,
so you may cease to be invisible,
so you may live without fear.

That all men are created equal.

—Declaration of Independence, 1776

The happy and the powerful do not go into exile.

—Alexis de Tocqueville, *Democracy in America*

Little is more extraordinary than the decision to migrate.

—John F. Kennedy, *A Nation of Immigrants*

We must take sides. Neutrality helps the oppressor, never the victim. . . . Action is the only remedy to indifference, the most insidious danger of all.

—Elie Wiesel, *Night*

The time to fix our broken immigration system is now.

—Barack Obama, May 23, 2007, U.S. Senate

CONTENTS

INTRODUCTION

Here is not merely a nation, but a teeming nation of nations.
—WALT WHITMAN, *Leaves of Grass*

Now is the time.

For millions of immigrants in the United States, their worst nightmare is becoming a reality.

President Barack Obama has not fulfilled his promise to create an immigration bill by the end of his first year in office. In fact, the rate of deportations has increased since the Bush administration. During fiscal year 2009, 387,790 immigrants were deported or left the United States voluntarily. Even worse, anti-immigrant sentiment in this country continues to grow.

Arizona has become ground zero in the immigration debate. On April 23, 2010, Governor Jan Brewer signed SB 1070, creating a law that, according to its critics, amounts to institutionalizing the practice of racial profiling—in other words, legalized racism. This law makes it a state crime for any person to be unable to produce proof of citizenship at all times, or to provide aid or transportation to an undocumented immigrant. It also authorizes the police to act as immigration agents by detaining anyone they suspect may be living in this country illegally. This is, unquestionably, the most anti-immigrant legislation in the United States. If there is any silver lining to what happened in Arizona, it is that the issue of immigration reform has been placed front and center on the national stage with a renewed sense of urgency. The possibility that similar laws might be passed in other states has reignited the immigration debate nationwide.

The Arizona law reveals that discrimination is still present in our so-called postracial society. It also means that the Republicans who favored the bill haven't learned from their electoral mistakes and Hispanics will continue to vote against them.

Any immigration reform requires presidential leadership. But there is a growing sense of grievance in the Latino community toward Obama. Many Hispanics believe that if the president had fought for immigration reform with the same determination he showed during the health care debate, Arizona might never have signed SB 1070 into law. President Obama has described it as "misguided" and even many Republicans have expressed serious concerns about it. The fact is, SB 1070 is Arizona's response to the federal government's inaction.

Both parties have said time and again that the immigration system is broken but neither has made a substantial effort to pass a bill. In early 2010, Representative Luis Gutierrez (D-Ill), and Senators Harry Reid (D-NV),

Charles Schumer (D-NY), Bob Menendez (D-NJ), and Lindsey Graham (R-SC) presented three different immigration frameworks. All three included new enforcement rules and a path to citizenship. However, none of the frameworks had the support of the Republican Party or the votes to pass in either chamber of Congress.

Politics prevailed and nothing was done.

The U.S. immigration system is unsustainable. We have waited for two decades for some kind of real reform.

And we are still waiting.

The life of Alfredo Quiñones-Hinojosa is an inspiring example of what an undocumented immigrant can do in the United States when given the opportunity.

Alfredo came to the United States as an undocumented immigrant in 1987. He was just nineteen years old, and one of six children. "I was hopping back and forth," he told me, "between Calexico (in the United States) and Mexicali (in Mexico). . . . All I wanted to do back then was provide food and basic living essentials to a very poor Mexican family."

Alfredo crossed over the border without the aid of a coyote, or guide. His family didn't have the six-hundred-dollar going rate to hire one at the time.

His first job was as a farmhand, cultivating tomatoes, chili peppers, and cotton in central California's San Joaquin Valley. He earned $3.35 an hour. Later, he moved to a small city, where he tried his hand at other jobs:

sweeping floors, shoeing horses, and soldering metal. That was where he learned English, and eventually he applied and was accepted to a local community college.

His next big step was when he accepted an offer to study at the University of California at Berkeley. Alfredo dreamed of becoming a doctor, and nothing was going to stop him.

His grandmother in Mexico had been a midwife and an herbal healer, and it was she who inspired his interest in medicine. "I've had many examples to follow in my life, but I know she played a very important part," he remarked. "My grandmother was an incredibly respected person, not just by her friends and family, but also in that little agricultural community that existed there on the outskirts of Mexicali, in Baja California."

After graduating from Berkeley, Alfredo was accepted to Harvard Medical School, where he graduated with honors. He then returned to California to complete his residency in neurosurgery at the University of California– San Francisco.

"Remember," he made a point of saying, "Cesar Chavez said that one of the main problems we face is the fear of failure. We don't have to be afraid of failure. And I didn't have anything to lose." This young man, who started his working life harvesting cotton in the fields, now serves as the director of the brain tumor program at the Johns Hopkins Bayview campus.

After enduring a lengthy legal process, Alfredo became an American citizen in 1997. And in Boston, during his citizenship ceremony, he came to the realization that in a short time he had achieved something that takes most others an entire generation.

"The person who was speaking at the ceremony began to talk about how his great-grandfather had come here from Italy, and that his grandfather had worked hard so that his father could become a teacher, and how he eventually got to Harvard," he recalled. "And I realized that in less than ten years, I had jumped over all those generations."

As he told me, "A jump like that might seem incredible, but it's not impossible."

And what was the secret to his success? "Dedication, determination, discipline, dreams, and the support of many people, including my parents, especially," he replied. And one country, the United States, which offered Alfredo an opportunity he never could have found in his native Mexico.

Today, Alfredo's expertise in treating spinal, brain stem, and brain tumors quite literally saves lives. Every single day. He is also heavily involved in researching the origins of tumors, and in developing new ways of treating brain cancer that might one day lead to a cure. "That would be my dream," he said. "Of course, many people consider that impossible. But that's also what people would have said about my life, back when I was only nineteen years old," and an undocumented farm worker.

When considering the potential of the undocumented worker in the United States, remember Dr. Quiñones-Hinojosa's hands, which have made the long journey from the fields to the operating room. "Think about it," he said to me enthusiastically. "These same hands that were once picking tomatoes and chili peppers now touch the brains of my patients."

There are many people like Dr. Quiñones-Hinojosa living among us, and with as much potential. But so many are not as lucky as he is.

These millions continue to live in the shadows.

My goal in writing this book is to make the invisible visible, and to give voice to the voiceless.

In moments of economic crisis such as the one we are currently experiencing, when millions of people have lost their jobs and so many can barely afford life's necessities, fighting for major reforms to current policy—including the legalization of millions of undocumented immigrants—might seem like a wishful dream, destined for failure. But this dream can't fail. It must not.

More than at any other time in our nation's history, we have arrived at the perfect moment to show the world at large, as well as many of its own citizens, that the United States of America is itself an ideal, based on the promise that it is a nation of equals. Those of us living in this "land of opportunity" must embrace the notion that this country's greatness can be realized only if we respect who we *all* are and where we've *all* come from. For most of us, our families' roots spread well beyond this country's shores and borders.

The historic election of Barack Obama as our president offers us the ideal opportunity to allow those who live with fear, in the margins and shadows of society, to openly join the greater United States of America and its purposeful march toward a common good. At this crucial moment, we must not discount the ingenuity and strong work ethic of our immigrant communities. Obama is a perfect example of how the United States truly is a place where dreams can be fulfilled, regardless of one's race, religion, or ethnic background. But so many of us don't take advantage of these opportunities. Many people are so busy fighting for their right to exist in this country that they are unable to contribute their talents to making it even greater.

Some Americans can't help but ask, "Why, when I or someone in my family has lost their job, or is in danger of losing it, should I support the legalization of more workers?" Or, "Why would I encourage a newly arrived foreigner to compete with me for a job?"

These are valid questions. This book offers a response to these questions, and many others.

But I must begin by reminding the reader that the United States is a better nation because of the immigrants, both legal and otherwise, who had the courage to come here and attempt to build a prosperous life for themselves and their children. This nation was founded by immigrants. The Industrial Revolution and many other technological and cultural advances could not have taken place without immigrants betting that, if they worked hard enough, their future in this country would be a bright one. The United States would not be what it is today without the energy and creativity generated by immigrants with *and* without documentation. They are truly indispensable to the fabric of the nation, and are key components of its future success.

In the next few pages, I will outline the enormous contributions that undocumented immigrants have made to this country, and I'll show why—despite so much criticism to the contrary—they should be legalized. I'll attempt to illustrate this point through facts and logic, without all the destructive rhetoric and divisiveness that have come to define this debate.

I'm not alone in my opinion.

Politicians from both parties have argued in favor of legalization for years. And yet both parties remain at an impasse. Undocumented immigration has become such a large problem that we can no longer continue to put off the debate. It is essential that we engage in an honest and respectful discourse in order to arrive at a realistic resolution to this pressing issue.

The time is now.

Never in U.S. history have there been so many undocumented immigrants whose rights must first be established and subsequently upheld. Creating new laws to protect undocumented immigrants in this country is a new frontier in civil rights. Never has the extraordinary American tradition of integrating newly arrived immigrants into our society been put to such a difficult test. There have never been more punitive laws, and repercussions for disobeying those laws, in place—from the local all the way to the federal level—designed to inhibit immigrants' ability to assimilate and prosper. The future of the United States depends upon our finding constructive alternatives to these measures. A nation as diverse as ours is obligated to preserve the values of equality and tolerance upon which it was founded.

In this time of economic crisis, compounded by the ongoing fight against terrorism, the first impulse is often to blame immigrants for many of society's problems. But this impulse must be countered through logic and reasoning, and by reenergizing the generosity that this country has historically shown to foreigners.

The United States draws its unrivaled strength from the diversity of its people, its tolerance for those who are different, and its talent for finding innovative routes to future success. Those who say that this country's ability to succeed is dependent on a single language—or worse, a shared perception that being American is signified by the physical features of its citizens—show a poor grasp of history and an even poorer instinct for the future. The unity that defines this nation is the result of shared values and the marvelous concept, established in the Declaration of Independence, that all men and women are created equal. We speak many languages, come in all colors, and believe very strongly that our future lies in this great land.

One cannot deny that the debate over undocumented immigrants is rife with heated passions and intense controversy. At times it seems that there is no common ground whatsoever between those who desire legalization and those seeking deportation. But there are in fact several things that we should all be able to agree on:

- *We agree* that current U.S. immigration policy is broken and in desperate need of repair.
- *We agree* that nobody is in favor of *un*documented immigration (not even the undocumented immigrants themselves).
- *We agree* that the United States—like any country—has the right to defend its borders and establish a policy of who is allowed in and who is not.
- *We agree* that there is absolutely no justification for the ongoing death of countless immigrants in the regions along both sides of the border.
- *We agree* that U.S. policy should not break apart families.
- *We agree* that it is impossible to deport every single undocumented immigrant, which is why we must find a realistic option for those who are already here.

These six points of agreement will serve as our starting point.

But where do we go from here?

There are many opinions on this issue, from those hardliners who believe in the use of force, more raids, more Border Patrol agents, more deportations, and more anti-immigrant legislation; to those who feel that undocumented immigrants should be granted blanket citizenship, as put forth in the Immigration Reform and Control Act sponsored by former president Ronald Reagan in 1986.

From the outset, we can say that the simple use of force has not and will not, in and of itself, solve the immigration problem. It is physically impossible to arrest and deport 12 million men, women, and children. I can't even begin to imagine how it would appear to the rest of the world: police, immigration and customs agents, and military personnel forcibly carrying entire families off to detention centers, where they will be held indefinitely until they are eventually deported back to their countries of origin. It would not be tolerated. And it should not be. This is not who we are in the United States of America.

But we must also recognize that, faced with the current financial crisis and the growing anti-immigrant sentiment plaguing many communities, there is not enough political will in Washington to pass an immigration reform bill similar to the one that gave three million people proper documentation just over two decades ago. And such blanket reform, without adequate organization and planning, would not be a viable solution to our current immigration problem.

Our obligation now is to find a middle ground that is sufficiently flexible and effective to serve us at least through the end of this century. The United States is currently going through a demographic revolution, and what this country currently looks like is not how it will look as the twenty-first century ends.

We have to think long-term. Interim solutions aren't sufficient to deal with this sort of ongoing situation. And we must be realistic. As long as the United States is an economic superpower, millions of people from all across the globe will be looking for a way to live on its soil. In fact, we should probably start to worry when people *don't* dream of coming to the United States in search of a better life. So we must take the continuing desire of millions who want to live in the United States and address it in a way that benefits this country, rather than tears it apart.

Before this can happen, we must resolve the issue of those undocumented immigrants who are already here.

In the next few pages, I will examine the dilemma of the "invisibles," the undocumented immigrants currently living in the United States. And I will present ten concrete reasons, based on facts and statistics, that justify the legalization of these millions of people.

The immigrant situation must be considered within the context of the enormous growth of the Hispanic population in the United States, and its historic participation in the 2008 presidential election.

Finally, in addition to proposing some concrete solutions for the current immigration problem, I'll present a manifesto of sorts for a new United States of America. The United States will never be a truly united nation until it does everything within its power to end discrimination, and until it recognizes that the future strength of this country depends on its continuing the tradition of renewal in the form of immigrant waves.

The United States' destiny depends, in no small part, upon how it resolves this current immigrant crisis and finds a way to uphold the rights of the most vulnerable members of its society: the undocumented.

A COUNTRY FOR ALL

One

THE INVISIBLES

Nobody notices them.

Sometimes they pass right in front of us, and we look through them as if they were not there.

But they are here, and the United States would be a very different country without them. People don't realize just how important they are to our way of life.

Those who go through each day unseen are undocumented immigrants. *The invisibles*.

They go out of their way not to be noticed by authorities or counted by census takers. It's not always easy to distinguish exactly who is an immigration agent. In order to avoid the risk of making a mistake, they talk to no one.

They stay away from the police. The invisibles keep their distance from them, even though many times they need protection from the violence of those who want to do them harm. The less they're seen, the greater the chance that they will be left alone to work and earn their wages in peace.

They live in the shadows. Being seen is a great risk and could mean deportation from the country that they have called home for years, the country where their children were born and, for many, their grandchildren too.

They live in silence. They don't often complain, though they certainly have reasons to. Complaints lead to questions. Questions lead to trouble.

When we cross paths with them on the street, they quickly avert their eyes. Not being is their way of being. For them, not having an identity is their identity.

Nevertheless, the United States could not function without their labor. They do this country's most difficult, least desirable, lowest-paying work. They clean what nobody else will clean, harvest the crops no one will harvest, cook our food, and build our houses.

It's likely that you're hardly aware of their presence in hotels and restaurants. But they're there. They're like ghosts. They walk without making noise and speak only when it's absolutely essential for them to do so.

They work behind the scenes, in kitchens, doing anything from washing dishes to preparing the finest cuisine. They learn quickly, and they are adept at making things— anything—because they are determined to survive. Their getting through the day gives their children opportunities they never had.

They accept working conditions that no legal citizen can imagine. They don't have the benefit of minimum wage; it's unheard-of for most. They don't get health insurance, do not have labor organizations to support them, and operate under the perennial threat of being unjustly fired or reported to Immigration Services and thus deported—often forced to leave children behind.

They clean up after us in public bathrooms, spending as many as ten hours a day steeped in filth for virtually no money. And though they are taken advantage of by so many, they continue to believe in the dreams that brought them here.

Without them our lives would be far less comfortable.

They are forced to sleep in trailers, or entire families are piled into a single bedroom. Mom, dad, and the children share a single ramshackle bed, because it's all they have. Many times they are forced to make room for an aunt or grandmother or the cousin of a neighbor's friend who just happens to show up one day. And they do so gladly, because to them family is all-important. They take care of their own. No one else will.

Despite all the negative things that are said about them—that they're criminals and terrorists—we let them into our homes, we allow them to clean up after us, and we even let them care for our children.

They are the nannies nurturing future presidents, governors, lawyers, doctors, mayors, actors, inventors, football players, Broadway and Hollywood stars. They care for the next generation so that these children's parents can work and go out at night.

They take our children to the park, they feed them, they protect them, and they care for them as if they were their own, because—as is so often the case—circumstances made it necessary for them to leave their children behind in their home country. It may be only a few hours away by plane, or a phone card or a mouse click away, but for these immigrants their children might as well be on another planet.

They're here because they were dying of hunger in their countries of origin, or because they don't want to condemn their children to the lives of poverty that their parents and grandparents had no choice but to endure. They came here in search of opportunities that are absent in their native lands. And that is exactly why, even though many Americans don't realize that they exist, these immigrants are the strongest, bravest, most innovative, most persistent, most courageous, most devoted individuals you will ever meet. And each is fully committed to doing whatever it takes to succeed in the United States.

But the cost is great. They *become* invisible. And now the time has come to offer them the recognition, respect, and, eventually, the visibility they deserve: the opportunity to coexist with us.

There is no better source of self-esteem than being seen, and being recognized for your labor, without feeling fear and without being forced to avert your eyes.

It's difficult to estimate exactly how many undocumented immigrants are currently living in the United States, precisely because they are undocumented. But the Pew Hispanic Center offers the most realistic statistics: nearly 12 million.[1]

The undocumented immigrant population continues to grow: In 2000, it was 8.4 million; in 2004, 10.2 million; and in 2008, 11.9 million.

On average, 450,000 undocumented immigrants arrived each year between 2000 and 2004. This figure dropped to 425,000 per year between 2004 and 2008. Without a doubt, the U.S. economic crisis, coupled with the rise of anti-immigration measures, has had an impact on the number of people who are coming here for work.

The number of undocumented immigrants living in the United States fell to 10.8 million people in 2009, according to the Department of Homeland Security's Office of Immigration Statistics. But this number will grow again as soon as there is a solid economic recovery in the United States. It won't take long for news of such a recovery to reach the many Latin Americans looking for work. A new immigration wave is coming soon and the United States is not ready for it.

Increasingly, police across the country are being forced to act not only as local law enforcement but also as immigration agents. And there is a growing effort to criminalize the undocumented.

The 1996 passage of the Illegal Immigration Reform and Immigrant Responsibility Act increased the reasons for deportation, increased the penalties for immigrants found in the United States without legal documentation, and generally made the life of undocumented workers, who beyond being undocumented are not criminals, much more difficult.

Instead of simply calling for the arrest and deportation of

undocumented workers, this act encouraged that they be
charged with additional crimes such as falsifying documents, making their already fragile legal situation even more
difficult. This can mean months and even years in prison
before they are actually deported back to the countries of
their birth. Not only does this cause a great deal of suffering
for the immigrants themselves, but prosecuting and jailing
them costs the United States an untold amount of money.

Every year it gets harder to find work and becomes
more likely that families will be torn apart, yet they continue to come.

Even with the reduced numbers of undocumented
immigrants, for every one deported out of the United
States, at least one more is entering. What sort of immigration policy is this? It could be described many ways,
but *efficient* and *inexpensive* are not among them.

On average, one undocumented immigrant enters the
country every minute.

One per minute.

Hunger is stronger than fear.

Undocumented immigration follows the simple economic relationship between supply and demand. As long
as unemployment remains high and pay remains low
in Mexico, Latin America, and developing countries
throughout the world and work continues to be available
in the United States, where one can earn five dollars an
hour rather than five dollars a day, undocumented immigration will continue to be a problem.

The vast majority—four out of five—of undocumented immigrants leave Latin America for the United States. And out of the 9.6 million undocumented Latinos estimated to have been in the United States in March of 2008, seven million were from Mexico.

Fifty-nine percent of all undocumented immigrants are from Mexico, 22 percent are from other Latin American nations, 12 percent are from Asia, 4 percent come from Europe and Canada, and the remaining 4 percent are from Africa and other areas around the globe.[2]

Clearly, U.S. immigration policy is not working. According to the Pew Hispanic Center, undocumented immigrants represented one-third of the roughly 39 million foreign-born people living in the United States in 2008. Their numbers are growing at a prodigious rate, with an increase of 5.3 million since the year 2000.

We are so accustomed to turning a blind eye to these workers that even Michael Chertoff, the Homeland Security secretary under George W. Bush and the man responsible for administering U.S. immigration policy, failed to realize that undocumented immigrants were working in his own home.

According to a 2008 report by the *Washington Post*, five undocumented workers were employed by the service that cleaned Secretary Chertoff's house in Maryland for four years.[3] He paid $185 for their services every other week for *four* years.

Secret Service agents regularly reviewed the cleaning company's employees' identification and never reported any problems. This issue came to light only when U.S. Immigration and Customs Enforcement (ICE) agents discovered that the owner of the business had not properly verified his employees' documentation, nor had he filed since 1986 the necessary I-9 forms for reporting their income to the IRS. He was fined a total of $22,880.

Chertoff chose not to comment publicly on the issue. Were he and his wife responsible for confirming that no undocumented immigrants were working in their home? Legally, no. The cleaning company was required to verify that its employees' paperwork was in order. Nonetheless, the reality is that five undocumented immigrants regularly cleaned the house where Secretary Chertoff slept and went unnoticed for *four years*.

This goes to show that undocumented immigrants are an integral part of *everyone's* daily life in the United States, even those holding the highest positions in our government.

"This matter illustrates the need for comprehensive immigration reform and the importance of effective tools for companies to determine the lawful status of their workforce," affirmed Homeland Security spokesman Russ Knocke.[4]

Clearly. And if something like this could happen to Chertoff, what about the other 300 million Americans who aren't in charge of federal immigration policy and who don't have the benefit of the Secret Service, official investigations, and ICE agents to verify documentation?

In a speech in late 2008, Michael Chertoff triumphantly stated that one of his major achievements was "reversing the flow of illegal immigration."[5] He was referring to the fact that the number of undocumented immigrants crossing the border had shrunk, while the number of deportations had risen. A more positive achievement would have been to discourage undocumented immigration while finding a way to legalize the undocumented immigrants already living and working productively in the United States.

From the day that Chertoff took office as Homeland Security secretary on February 15, 2005, until he left that post on January 21, 2009, over one million undocumented immigrants entered the United States. (And I'm using the same statistics as the Pew Hispanic Center, which Chertoff mentioned in his speech.)

This does not sound like a "reversal" of the flow of undocumented immigration.

In the middle of 2007, with only a year and a half left before the presidential election, many people predicted that immigration would become one of the central themes of the campaign. At the same time, many in Congress were also thinking about reelection, or about protecting their political allies. Since immigration is so controversial, many politicians try dancing around the issue when seeking reelection. It was in that already highly charged environment that the Senate began debating the future of the 12 million invisibles.

The debate, of course, was doomed to continue to the present. The immense political difficulties surrounding this issue are illustrated by the fate of George W. Bush's efforts to reform U.S. immigration policy. President Bush arrived at the Oval Office in 2001 with the clear intention of fulfilling one of his campaign promises by finding a way to legalize undocumented immigrants. In fact, on July 10, 2001, during a ceremony on Ellis Island, the president made the following statement: "Immigration is not a problem to be solved. It is a sign of a confident and successful nation. . . . New arrivals should be greeted not with suspicion and resentment, but with openness and courtesy."

Despite the clear support of the president—who, during his 2000 campaign, promised to make the INS more "immigrant friendly," to cut application times for citizenship and green cards, and to encourage family reunification—by June 28, 2007, there were still not enough votes in the Senate to approve the legalization of undocumented immigrants. Only forty-six senators voted in favor of the proposed legislation. With fifty-three voting against it, there was no way for the bill to receive the sixty votes necessary to become law.

The invisibles remain invisible.

And mute.

To be clear, it was a bipartisan failure: fifteen Democrats, thirty-seven Republicans, and one Independent voted against the bill. President Bush himself admitted, in an interview with ABC near the end of his second term in office, that the impossibility of passing meaningful immigration reform was one of the biggest disappointments of his presidency.[6]

In the end, instead of legalizing undocumented workers, the Bush administration began stepping up its efforts to arrest and deport them. As the window of opportunity closed for these immigrants, it was a double blow: not only had their chance to become citizens disappeared before their eyes, but they were also faced with unprecedented persecution.

In 2008, the ICE deported 349,041 people,[7] a 20 percent increase from the previous year.[8] Despite this record number of deportations, the quantity of undocumented immigrants entering the country was higher still. In fact, there were more than ever.

The number of raids also swelled under the Bush administration, with federal agents rounding up immigrants from their homes or from the taquerias, factories, meatpacking plants, and painting companies where they worked. The immigrants caught in these raids were prosecuted in federal court, forced to give DNA samples, and detained for lengthy periods of time before deportation; they were treated, in many cases, as if they were accused terrorists. In fact, they are being prosecuted so vigorously that it has been a drain on the entire federal court system.

In 2002, only 510 arrests resulted from these seizures. In

2008 this number had soared to 6,287.[9] It's almost absurd (if it weren't so tragic) that in four days, the same number of undocumented workers will enter the country as were deported in the entire past year through raids.

The social consequences are devastating. "You have single mothers now," Illinois congressman Luis Gutierrez said in an NPR interview. "You have young, fifteen-year-old kids with no father. Think about that for a moment. And the government took your dad away."[10]

Clearly, workplace raids are not productive. For example, on the morning of March 6, 2007, around five hundred ICE agents entered a building in New Bedford, Massachusetts.

Over 320 immigrants were detained in a factory that produced leather goods to be used by the United States Army. These workers were manufacturing products that are vital to our soldiers.

The majority of those arrested were women from Guatemala and El Salvador, and most of them were put on a plane and flown to a detention center in Texas to await deportation.

Because of the raid, roughly one hundred children were left without a mother or a father to care for them. One hundred children, essentially orphaned. This number was confirmed by Corinn Williams, executive director of the Community Economic Development Center, who said, "It's been a widespread humanitarian crisis here in New Bedford."

According to the *Washington Post*, Keylyn Zusana

Lopez Ayala, an eight-month-old baby, was taken to the emergency room suffering from pneumonia and possible dehydration. Her mother had been detained and unable to breast-feed her.[11] There are many more stories like this.

Ultimately, some seventy undocumented immigrants had to be released because there was no one else who could care for their children.

What was gained from the raid in New Bedford? Did it solve Massachusetts's immigration problems? No. Will this raid prevent other undocumented workers from coming to the United States? No. Will it even stem the tide? No.

The only thing it accomplished was to instill terror in the immigrant community. Can you imagine a child's fear at never knowing whether his parents will come home from work each day? Can you imagine the trauma of being arrested and deported, unable to bring your infant with you? Not knowing what will become of your child?

And the people arrested in New Bedford—every single one of them—were hard workers. Not criminals, just women who were trying to make their way in the world. In the country that they viewed as a land of opportunity.

Initial reports indicated that those undocumented immigrants were doing jobs that no other Americans wanted to do. Federal investigators found that the employees had endured horrendous working conditions. They were allegedly docked twenty dollars for talking or for spending more than two minutes in the bathroom.

This is just one of numerous tragic cases.

✦

"Around four in the morning, I was awoken by someone pounding on my door," Walter told me. He thought he was late for work, and that it was a friend trying to make sure he was up. But it wasn't. "It was immigration. It was the police."

I met Walter in the summer of 2007 in a Virginia detention center for undocumented immigrants. The sun was just starting to rise after the worst night of his life. His voice and hands were trembling. He hadn't shaved or even brushed his teeth. His breath smelled of fear.

Walter had come to the United States from Bolivia to save a life. His wife, he told me, was suffering from lupus.

"I broke the law," he admitted during an interview in his cell. "But it was for a life. I am here to save a life. Not for anything else." His deportation, he assured me, would be tantamount to a "death sentence" for his wife. They just didn't have the money to pay for treatment.

In Bolivia, under Evo Morales's government, there aren't adequate medical facilities. Coming to the United States was his wife's only chance for survival. And that's exactly what they did.

Walter was simply in the wrong place at the wrong time.

ICE agents were looking for someone else. But when they found Walter instead and asked him about his immigration status, he showed the agents his Bolivian passport.

He was arrested and taken by van to the detention center, where they initiated deportation proceedings. His wife apparently was not in the house at the time.

During the first few hours after his detention, Walter hoped that he would be allowed to remain in the United States on humanitarian grounds. After all, there was a life at stake.

"The raids should be directed at people looking to harm this country," he told me, his voice heavy with resignation. "All we did was look for work. And try to get adequate medical care for my wife."

His pleas went unanswered. Walter was sent back to Bolivia shortly after our interview.

Even when these raids are specifically targeted at finding, arresting, detaining, and deporting criminals, they've proven to be largely ineffective. In the majority of cases, those who are captured have no criminal history whatsoever. A report by the independent Migration Policy Institute entitled "Collateral Damage: An Examination of ICE's Fugitive Operations Program" found that 73 percent of nearly 97,000 people arrested by ICE fugitive operations teams between the program's inception in 2003 and early 2008 were unauthorized immigrants *without* criminal records. Despite the National Fugitive Operations Program's mandate to apprehend dangerous fugitives, arrests of undocumented immigrants with criminal convictions have represented a steadily declining share of total arrests by the teams—accounting for just 9 percent of total arrests in 2007, down from 32 percent in 2003, according to the Department of Homeland Security's own estimate.[12]

These workplace raids are not an effective way to apprehend convicted criminal fugitives.

During his presidential campaign, Barack Obama criticized raids that broke apart families. "I don't believe it is the American way to grab a mother away from her child and deport her without us considering the consequences of that."[13]

The basic question is this: What is gained by annually deporting some six thousand of those arrested during raids at a cost of millions of dollars when thousands more will enter the country every year? Later, in an interview at the White House in mid-April 2009, Obama hadn't changed his mind about the raids. "I continue to believe that you can't raid your way out of the problem," he told me. "That is a shortcut; it is a symbolic step and it does not solve the underlying issues."

Of the 2.2 million immigrants deported between 1997 and 2007, more than 100,000 were fathers and mothers of children born in the United States. This is far from the "compassion" so many politicians say they represent. No one wins with such ineffective enforcement.

Not only do these raids and subsequent deportations terrorize the Latino community and tear apart thousands of Hispanic families, they also adversely affect U.S. citizens. According to a study conducted by the National Council of

La Raza and the Urban Institute, at least thirteen thousand children born in the United States saw either one or both of their parents deported between 2006 and 2007. Two-thirds of the children of undocumented immigrants are citizens by the simple fact of having been born on U.S. soil.[14] We are unnecessarily creating thousands of orphans who become the responsibility of the U.S. government. We unnecessarily make these children *our* responsibility.

One of the most dramatic cases was that of a twenty-six-year-old Honduran woman by the name of Saída Umanzor, who was arrested in her home in Conneaut, Ohio, on October 26, 2007, and held for eleven days. Her nine-month-old child, Brittney Bejarano, was still being breast-fed—her only source of nutrition—when her mother was arrested.

In this case, the then director of ICE, Julie Myers, intervened on their behalf, freeing the mother and reuniting her with her American child. Fortunately, Brittney survived the nearly two-week separation from her mother.

Unlike most of the thousands of families torn apart by U.S. immigration policy, Saída and Brittney's story has a happy ending. They were fortunate that a government official recognized the injustice of their situation. We need everyone to realize that separating families is no solution to undocumented immigration. In fact, it is detrimental to all parties.

✦

In January of 2009, with the help of attorneys, some six hundred children—the majority of whom were born in the United States—filed a suit with the Supreme Court seeking to halt the deportation of their undocumented parents. The lawsuit also named President Barack Obama.

"[Obama] is the only one who can sign an executive order stopping deportations . . . and stopping the tears and the pain of these children," Nora Sandigo told me during an interview. She is an attorney, and, as the executive director of the organization American Fraternity, she is acting as the children's advocate and legal guardian.

Among these young plaintiffs are Maricela Soza's two children. She was arrested in Miami, in her own home, by ICE agents. "I was there when it happened," nine-year-old Ronald Soza told me, recounting the moment when the officers entered the house. "I started to cry and ran to my room."

In a desperate attempt to stop their mother's deportation, Ronald and his twelve-year-old sister, Cecia, went on a hunger strike.

"I stopped eating for three days," Cecia told me. The children began their protest at the American Fraternity offices in Miami. Their father was not there, afraid that he too would be arrested by the ICE, thus leaving his two children in the United States without even one parent.

In the end, all the children's efforts were in vain.

On January, 28, 2009, after forty-two days of incarceration, Maricela Soza was deported to Nicaragua. "I don't know what's going to happen next," she told me tearfully from Managua. "I told my children to be very patient. I'm asking them to reopen the case; it's the only thing I can do."

Despite these heartbreaking stories of broken families, there are those who want to enforce the law with an even heavier hand.

In August of 2008, Texas congressman Lamar Smith wrote an open letter stating the following: "The current practice of birthright citizenship—granting automatic citizenship to children born to illegal immigrants on United States soil—creates a tremendous incentive for people to come here illegally and stay. America is the only industrialized nation that doesn't require at least one parent to be in the country legally before a child becomes a citizen. Congress should put an end to this practice."[15]

Unsurprisingly, the majority of Hispanics disagree with Congressman Smith. According to polls conducted for America's Voice and a postelection survey by the NALEO Educational Fund, ImpreMedia, and the Latino Decisions polling firm, "67 percent of all voters and 71 percent of Latino voters believe that illegal immigrants 'should be required to register and become legal' rather than leaving the country or being allowed to stay only temporarily."[16] Immigrants want to be documented; they want to stay here legally. Most of these people are not criminals, nor do they intend to become criminals in this country. They are simply people just like you or me, who are desperate to make a better life for themselves and their families in the United States. We should always remember how proud we are of the fact that living the American dream is a goal for people all over the world.

Study after study shows that Hispanics support ending the raids and legalizing the status of undocumented immigrants. And in 2008, the presidential candidates from both major parties realized very quickly that if they wanted to win the Latino vote, they would have to concede this point.

In an interview in Denver on May 28 of 2008, Barack Obama told me that, as president, he would revise current immigration policy, including the raids and the fence being erected along the border with Mexico. He added, "I cannot guarantee that it is going to be in the first hundred days, but what I can guarantee is that we will have in the first year an immigration bill that I strongly support."[17] It is a promise he has reiterated in the early months of his presidency.

John McCain took a more strident position. Before even considering a program to legalize undocumented immigrants, he wanted to secure the border and have the governors of the border states certify that significant progress had been made in reducing the amount of undocumented immigration. "So we can together, Republicans and Democrats, work out this issue, provide a path to citizenship on the principle that they do not take any priority over anyone who came to this country legally or waited legally," he told me.[18] This process would definitely take more than a year; in fact, it would probably take several years.

With these promises from Obama and McCain, Hispanics had achieved something very important: they have leveraged their political power so that millions of undocumented immigrants would have a chance of legalizing their status.

The same way that the Jewish community can call upon a candidate to defend the state of Israel, or that Cuban Americans can demand that their representatives take a position against the Castro regime, Latino voters across the country had obtained something very concrete and significant: a voice.

Ultimately, every Hispanic vote cast in the 2008 presidential election meant that an undocumented immigrant could eventually emerge from the shadows and leave behind the threat of future persecution.

In other words, each Hispanic vote was worth two. Nearly ten million Latinos voted in the election, and nearly ten million undocumented immigrants are that much closer to legalization.

Every Latino who voted represented an immigrant who couldn't.

The 2008 Hispanic vote wasn't free. It demanded something very important in return: the promise that the invisibles will be brought into the light.

Two

A NATION OF EQUALS

If anything characterizes the United States, it's the promise that every single one of us will be treated equally. This nation represents incomparable opportunity, something unique in a largely unfair world.

No other country has offered such hope: the idea that anyone can come here, work hard, and make a good life. But the truly incredible thing about the experiment that is the United States of America is the diversity of its citizens.

The U.S. Census Bureau is forecasting that, in less than thirty years, this will be a minority-majority country. Very shortly, the U.S. will no longer have just one majority ethnic group, as evidenced by the impressive demographic growth of the Hispanic and Asian populations in recent years. These two groups—along with African Americans and native or indigenous peoples—will see their numbers and power continue to grow.

Despite the vast differences in racial, ethnic, and religious origins existent in the U.S. population, we are all expected to embody the conviction that nobody is superior to anyone else and nobody is inferior. This is different from saying that our society is completely without prejudice (sadly, such a thing doesn't exist yet), but it is a society based on the constitutional right to equal treatment and protection under the law.

In 1776, the Declaration of Independence established that, "We hold these truths to be self-evident, that all men are created equal, that they are endowed by their Creator with certain unalienable Rights, that among these are Life, Liberty and the pursuit of Happiness."

This affirmation is a wonderful example of the extraordinary power of words and ideas. The supremely compelling notion that "all men are created equal" was, and continues to be, the inspiration that is this superpower's foundation.

The force of this concept is reiterated in Article 1 of the Universal Declaration of Human Rights, approved by the General Assembly of the United Nations in 1948: "All human beings are born free and equal in dignity and rights."[1]

The young French traveler Alexis de Tocqueville visited the United States in 1831. During his stay he realized that this new nation was overwhelmingly characterized by its belief in equality. "In the United States, nothing struck me more forcibly than the general equality of condition among the people," he wrote in *Democracy in America*. "The more I advance in the study of the American society, the more I perceive that this equality of condition is the fundamental fact from which all others seem to be derived."[2]

Equality. The potent energy of the American experiment radiates from this source. And decades later, the Declaration of Independence provided the inspiration for the abolition of slavery.

It is, of course, ironic that Thomas Jefferson—who included the phrase "all men are created equal" in this document—was himself a slave owner and fathered a number of children with one of his slaves, a woman by the name of Sally Hemmings.

In October of 1854, in Peoria, Abraham Lincoln gave a speech reminding the country that it was founded on the concept of equality for all, and he called for the freeing of the slaves:

> Near eighty years ago we began by declaring that all men are created equal; but now from that beginning we have run down to the other declaration, that for some men to enslave others is a 'sacred right of self-government.' . . . Our republican robe is soiled and trailed in the dust. Let us re-purify it. . . . Let us re-adopt the *Declaration of Independence*.[3]

The United States had to suffer a devastating civil war in order to finally end slavery in 1865, and it wasn't until 1870 that African Americans, though freed from their chains, earned the right to vote. It would be nearly a century before society caught up to the law and these former slaves were fully able to exercise this right.

The election of Barack Obama as the first African American president of the United States, on November 4, 2008, signifies a historic milestone for a country that accepted slavery for nearly one hundred years and that—even today—continues to battle racism in many forms.

Obama personifies the words in the Reverend Dr. Martin Luther King Jr.'s famous 1963 speech in which he said, "I have a dream that one day this nation will rise up and live out the true meaning of its creed: 'We hold these truths to be self-evident: that all men are created equal.' . . . I have a dream that my four little children will one day live in a nation where they will not be judged by the color of their skin but by the content of their character."[4]

Today, more than 230 years after the Declaration of Independence and more than forty years after Dr. King's speech, we find ourselves once again reminding the United States of its belief that "all men [and women] are created equal" by demanding equal treatment for immigrants and the legalization of millions of undocumented workers.

It is difficult to imagine that millions of people could be living under conditions that—in the extreme—approach those of slavery in this, the most powerful nation in the world.

Yet they are.

The greatness of nations is judged not by the way they

treat the richest and most powerful of its citizens; rather, it is judged by the way they treat the poorest and most vulnerable. And today, without a doubt, undocumented immigrants are the most vulnerable people living in the United States.

George Washington, the first U.S. president, understood this tenet perfectly when he said, "The bosom of America is open to receive not only the opulent and respectable stranger, but the oppressed and persecuted of all nations and religions; whom we shall welcome to a participation of all our rights and privileges. . . ."

The United States is not a nation composed of immigrants; rather it is a nation created by immigrants. Every family living here came from other shores. Every single person in the U.S. has at least one immigrant in his or her heritage.

Even Native Americans have their roots in another continent. The very first immigrants came to North America via the Bering Strait some thirty thousand years ago.

History shows us that even after Columbus the first colonizers of what we now call the United States were not English. Well before the founding of the English colonies Jamestown (1607) and Plymouth (1620), the Spanish created the San Agustín settlement in Florida in 1565. Other Spanish settlements existed in modern-day Texas and New Mexico through the end of the sixteenth century.

In the United States, nobody is "from here." We all originated somewhere else—a fact that we should take pains to remember again and again.

＊

Historically, the United States has been ambivalent when it comes to immigrants. In certain periods, the philosophy of the immigrant tradition that built this nation has prevailed, and the country has been generous and open. At other times, the United States has allowed irrational fears to take over, and the nation has given in to xenophobia and nativism, the fear of people from other places and the incorrect belief that getting here first earns one rights that those who come later don't deserve. As the worldwide population grows and economic competition increases, it's easy to become territorial in a way that is ultimately detrimental to society.

We should all be mindful of the fact that if immigration laws had always been as stringent as they are today, many American citizens' relatives would not have been able to enter this country. We would have missed out on an untold number of brilliant minds and so much cultural diversity without these earlier immigrant waves.

Prior to the nation's first immigration law in 1882, there were very few bureaucratic barriers set up to prevent people from entering the country. According to a report by the Immigration Policy Center, "many of our ancestors would not have qualified under today's immigration laws. . . . Until the late nineteenth century, there was very little federal regulation of immigration—there were virtually no laws to break. . . . Before the twentieth century, there was virtually no bureaucracy responsible for enforcing immigration laws. . . . Prior to the 1920s, there were no numerical limitations on immigration to the U.S., but certain persons were banned from entering."[5]

Despite fewer regulations, certain groups of new immigrants have been consistently rejected throughout the history of this country, particularly based on race or language.

Today, those immigrants are primarily Latin Americans. But they aren't the first to have been singled out.

In 1882, there was the Chinese Exclusion Act. This was the United States' first significant restriction on immigration, and it was provoked by the weak postwar economy and competition over gold mines in California. The act was meant to last for ten years; it banned Chinese workers from entering the country and made it illegal for those already here to stay. In 1921, the Quota Law placed numeric limitations on immigrants from certain countries—numbers that corresponded to their relative percentages of the overall population—benefiting Europeans at the expense of people from the rest of the world.[6]

Although these discriminatory views were written into law, the rejection of certain groups in the United States has primarily risen from societal attitudes.

In his 1751 book, *Observations*, Benjamin Franklin complained about the presence of tens of thousands of German immigrants in the Northeastern United States. "Why should Pennsylvania, founded by the English, become a Colony of Aliens, who will shortly be so numerous as to Germanize us instead of our Anglifying them, and will

never adopt our Language or Customs, any more than
they can acquire our Complexion."

Apparently, intelligence is no guarantee against prejudice. It's interesting to note that even today, people continue to use the same derogatory word Franklin did to
refer to immigrants: *aliens*. And his fear that their presence
would "Germanize" the United States has, in today's climate, become the fear of being "Latinized."

After the assimilation of the Germans (despite Franklin's
fears to the contrary), it was the Irish who faced rejection.
Fleeing hunger and extreme poverty, millions of Irish
immigrants arrived on American shores in the nineteenth
century.

The signs that went up in the windows of many businesses—NO IRISH NEED APPLY—speak volumes about the
attitudes toward Irish immigrants. And such bold racism
persisted well into the twentieth century toward other
nationalities. The revered Mexican American scholar
Julian Samora recounted traveling through Colorado in
the early forties as he interviewed for graduate school. He
was frequently turned away from hotels by signs that read
NO DOGS, INDIANS, OR MEXICANS ALLOWED.

And the Irish were followed by the Swedes—roughly a
million immigrated between 1840 and 1930. Next came the
Danes, the Norwegians, and the Finns.

Over four million Italians arrived on American shores
between 1880 and 1960. And they were followed by Poles,
Greeks, Czechs, Russians, and citizens of other European
nations.

Finally, a new law enacted in 1965 radically changed the nationality of the people settling in the United States. It would become perhaps the single most influential law in terms of defining the future demographics of this nation.

The limitations based on national origin were dismantled and instead the ability to work and family reunification were emphasized; as a result the faces of newly arrived immigrants began to change.

Before the Immigration Act of 1965, 85 percent of the population was white and generally of European descent. By the 1990s the percentage of immigrants hailing from Europe had been reduced to 16 percent. Instead, over half of all immigrants were coming from Latin America, and nearly a third were coming from Asia.[7]

In other words, a nation that had been mostly white and European—and operating under immigration laws that were set to ensure this would continue to be the case—was transformed into a country characterized by racial and ethnic diversity. And it's all thanks to President John F. Kennedy, whose commitment to immigrants is one of his underappreciated legacies.

Because of his tragic assassination in Dallas on November 22, 1963, Kennedy was never able to enact the new legislation he had worked so hard to create. But he was able to lay the groundwork for the demographic transformation of the United States of America, a vision he outlined in his 1958 book, *A Nation of Immigrants*. In just over fifty pages, Kennedy brilliantly summarized the history of immigration in the United States, and argued for expanding immigration and for equal treatment of those who come.

"This is the spirit which so impressed Alexis de Tocqueville and which he called the spirit of equality," he wrote. "It has meant that in a democratic society there should be no inequalities in opportunities or in freedoms."

In Kennedy's opinion, there is nothing in the Constitution calling for immigrants to be treated differently from natural-born citizens. Everyone must be treated equally under the law, and immigration policy must also reflect that view: "Immigration policy should be generous; it should be fair; it should be flexible. With such a policy we can turn to the world and to our own past, with clean hands and a clear conscience."

The president's brother, Robert Kennedy, also had a very clear vision for the United States. Shortly before he was assassinated in 1968, during his campaign for president, he spoke of "a great country, a selfless country, a compassionate country."

The great-great-grandparents of John, Robert, and Senator Edward Kennedy came from Ireland and sailed across the Atlantic Ocean to Boston a century and a half ago. Without immigration, the United States would not have the Kennedys, a family that continues to produce dedicated public servants.

"There is no question that the immigration system needs to be reformed to meet the challenges of the twenty-first century," Senator Edward Kennedy wrote in his introduction to the fiftieth-anniversary edition of *A*

Nation of Immigrants. "The urgent issue before us is about the future of America. It is about being proud of our immigrant past and our immigrant future. We know the high price of continuing inaction. Raids and other enforcement actions will escalate, terrorizing our communities and businesses. The twelve million undocumented immigrants now in our country will become millions more."

The year 1958, when *A Nation of Immigrants* was first published, is particularly significant to me. Who would have thought that the same year I was born in Mexico City, a senator from Massachusetts with presidential aspirations would publish a book that, decades later, opened the doors of the United States to me?

The United States is at a crucial moment in its history: it must decide whether to affirm its tradition of dignity and openness by legalizing immigrants and extending to them the same rights enjoyed by everyone who lives within its borders, or turn its back on history, renounce its own past, and be condemned to isolation, prejudice, and failure.

The United States must choose: respect and reinforce its tradition of welcoming newcomers to its shores, or close itself off and live in a form of apartheid.

Just as other groups—African Americans, Native Americans, women, and homosexuals—have fought for their rights, now is the time for immigrants to reaffirm the belief that, in this nation, everyone is truly equal.

This notion is beautifully captured in the words of the

poet Emma Lazarus that are inscribed on the Statue of Liberty in New York Harbor:

> *Give me your tired, your poor,*
> *Your huddled masses yearning to breathe free. . . .*

The United States owes its greatness, its status as a world power, to immigrants. And this is no time to change course.

After learning about the mistreatment of a foreign visitor in a store, Oprah Winfrey posed the following question on her popular daytime talk show: "Have we become a country in which only if you are American you receive fair treatment?"[8] The answer has yet to be determined. The answer is up to each and every one of us.

"We the People of the United States," the first line of the Preamble to the U.S. Constitution, can be interpreted in many ways. It guarantees justice, tranquillity, protection, welfare, and liberty to everyone who finds him- or herself within our borders. The Constitution does not specify that these rights apply only to those who carry U.S. passports or green cards.

The United States was founded on the idea that everyone must be treated equally, and the Constitution commits this intention to law. But there can be no doubt that today undocumented immigrants are not considered equal in this country. They consistently suffer persecution, their rights are violated, and their liberty is restricted.

The Founding Fathers sought to escape these very conditions when they signed the Declaration of Independence in 1776 and the Constitution in 1787.

Now it is up to us to make the necessary changes, ensuring that the United States continues to be a country in which all men and women are considered equal, regardless of race, religion, or immigration status.

Three

TEN REASONS FOR IMMIGRATION REFORM

There are at least ten reasons why we, as a nation, should legalize the status of the millions of undocumented immigrants in the United States:

1. Because the Declaration of Independence asserts that we are all equal.

2. Because immigrants—both documented and undocumented—are an important asset to the United States.

3. Because increasingly, immigrants will be needed to replace a retiring workforce.

4. Because the border fence will never effectively prevent undocumented immigrants from entering the country.

5. Because it's important that the children of undocumented adults have access to a solid education.

6. Because immigration is an economic problem that requires an economic solution.

7. Because it is the best way to help developing countries.

8. Because it will make the United States a safer place.

9. Because Barack Obama promised it.

10. Because the United States of America is a nation of immigrants.

1. Because the Declaration of Independence asserts that we are all equal.

"That all men are created equal." It is one of the most influential and powerful statements in any legal document in history. It is clear. It is direct. And it is absolute.

The Declaration of Independence, signed on July 4, 1776, does not state that occasionally some men and women are inferior to others. Nor does it specify that only those people who are born in the United States or have visas and green cards are created equal. No. It says that all people—all of them—are created equal.

The Declaration of Independence does not distinguish between citizens and noncitizens. In *A Nation of Immigrants*, President Kennedy himself points out that of the fifty-six signatures on that document, eight belonged to immigrants. It is clear that the Declaration was intended to include everyone, citizens and immigrants alike.

There are a number of things that we consider quintessentially "American" that, in fact, were originated by immigrants. Kennedy points out that Thomas Jefferson's prophetic words—"that all men are created equal"—were originally penned by an Italian national, Filippo Mazzei, in his writings on the American colonies. Jefferson and Mazzei were close friends. Even the name of the country itself—the United States of America—was borrowed from a Dutch republic known as the United States of the Netherlands.

This nation was established on an incontrovertible call for equality. It isn't important where you come from; it is your decision to make the United States your permanent home that really matters.

America was created by people fleeing political and religious persecution and by people seeking better economic opportunities. This has been the case for the past 230 years, and there is no reason to change it now.

2. Because immigrants—both documented and undocumented—are an important asset to the United States.

Undocumented immigrants are not criminals or terrorists. They bring infinitely more benefits to the United States than they receive in services. Contrary to popular belief, many undocumented immigrants do pay income taxes, and the majority would be willing to if they were fully integrated into the tax system. Even those who work off the books pay consumer taxes, and their employers often retain taxes from their paychecks. Undocumented immigrants create jobs, they do the work that most people have no desire to do, they keep inflation low, they harvest our crops, and they build our homes. Of course, they broke the law by coming here without proper processing, but these laws are also broken by the millions of American citizens and thousands of American businesses who hire them. While these employers take advantage of the benefits of their labor, only the immigrants suffer imprisonment and deportation. They pay into Social Security whether or not they ever receive money from it (in most cases they don't). They are allies in the fight against terrorism. They have as much or more faith than any citizen in the opportunities that the United States offers. They reinforce strong family values. They firmly believe that education is necessary for success. They diversify the population. Their native languages enrich the United States, and they learn English quickly. Their very presence promotes tolerance. They're even prepared to die for this country (sixty-five thousand immigrants have fought or are fighting in Iraq and Afghanistan, as of May 2008). All things considered, the positive influence that immigrants have on the United States greatly outweighs any negative aspects, as many studies have documented.

The most comprehensive report, weighing what immigrants contribute *to* and receive *from* society, was made by a panel of the National Research Council. In this study, the U.S. Commission on Immigration Reform, a congressionally appointed body, asked the Research Council (the principal operating arm of the National Academy of Sciences) "to examine the effects of immigration on the national economy, on government revenues and spending, and on the future size and makeup of the nation's population."

The study, entitled *The New Americans: Economic,*

Demographic, and Fiscal Effects of Immigration, was released
on May 17, 1997. And it concluded that immigrants—
regardless of their legal status—contribute more to this
country than they take away.

"Immigrants may be adding as much as $10 billion to
the economy each year," said James P. Smith, a senior
economist at RAND Corporation and one of the panel
chairs. "The vast majority of Americans are enjoying a
healthier economy as the result of the increased supply of
labor and lower prices that result from immigration."

The legalization of ten million immigrants or more
would bring enormous benefits to the economy of the
United States. Such a boost to the economy occurred
when the Immigration Reform and Control Act of 1986
was passed. "That legislation [1986] came about in the
middle of a financial downturn, when unemployment was
on the rise. What's interesting is that while the economy
fell and we found ourselves in a recession, taxes on the
recently legalized undocumented immigrants helped contribute to the economy."[1]

In August 2009 The Cato Institute concluded that the
legalization of undocumented immigrants "would improve
wages and working conditions for all workers." The following are their two most important conclusions:

1. A program to grant legal status to unauthorized
workers already in the United States, combined with new
channels for the arrival of immigrant workers in the future,
would increase the productivity of immigrant workers

and create more job openings for American workers in higher-skilled occupations. The net result would be economic gains in roughly $180 billion over ten years.

2. An enforcement-only approach would shrink the overall economy, reducing opportunities for higher-skilled American workers. The net result would be economic losses of roughly $80 billion over ten years.

Professor Raul Hinojosa-Ojeda of UCLA concluded in a study for the William C. Velasquez Institute that broad reform of immigration policy could generate between $4.5 billion and $5.4 billion in new tax revenue, and the creation of between 750,000 and 900,000 jobs (as reported by America's Voice on March 25, 2009).

Such statistics were supported by numbers released by the Immigration Policy Center, which concluded the following:

Legalization increases government revenues by bringing more workers into the tax system. . . . An "underground" labor force represents lost tax revenue. . . . Between one-half and three-quarters of undocumented immigrants now work "on the books" and pay federal and state income taxes, Social Security taxes and Medicare taxes. But as the 2005 Economic Report of the President points out, they "are ineligible for almost all Federal public assistance programs and most major Federal-state programs."

Workers with legal status earn and spend more.

Enforcement-only policies are expensive and ineffective.

Legalization increases immigration's economic benefits. . . . A 2007 report from the White House Council of Economic Advisers concluded that immigration as a whole increases the U.S. Gross Domestic Product (GDP) by roughly $37 million each year. . . . Immigrants do not compete with the majority of natives for the same jobs. . . . Immigrants usually "complement" the native-born workforce. . . . Immigrant businesses create jobs: In 2002, 1.6 million Hispanic-owned firms provided jobs to 1.5 million employees, had receipts of $222 billion, and generated payroll of $36.7 billion.

Of course, undocumented workers do cost the United States something. I'm well aware that one of the primary arguments against the legalization of undocumented immigrants is that they are a significant drain on educational costs and public health services. But layered within these arguments are a number of misconceptions.

Let's look at California, home to the majority of the country's undocumented immigrants. There is no way to accurately measure whether these immigrants are any greater strain on public health services than the increasing number of uninsured American citizens.

A study by the University of California's School of Public Health found that undocumented Mexicans visit the doctor less every year than people born in the United States to Mexican parents.[2]

According to that study, "Illegal Latino immigrants do not cause a drag on the U.S. health care system as some critics have contended and in fact receive less care than Latinos in the country legally, researchers said. . . . Low rates of use of health care services by Mexican immigrants . . . do not support public concern about immigrants' overuse of the health care system," the researchers wrote. "Undocumented individuals demonstrate less use of health care than U.S. born citizens." These findings coincide with those of the National Research Council. In the final analysis, the economic surplus created by undocumented immigrants is more than $10 billion a year.

The reality is that "recent immigrants were responsible for only about one percent of public medical expenditure, even though they constituted five percent of the population," according to a study published by the *American Journal of Public Health.* "Immigrants' medical costs averaged about 14 percent to 20 percent less than those who were U.S. born."

Many people believe undocumented immigrants and their children abuse the emergency rooms in this country but the Kaiser Commission found otherwise. The Immigration Policy Center reported, "Contrary to popular belief, noncitizens are significantly less likely to use emergency room services than U.S. citizens. In 2006, 20 percent of U.S.-citizen adults and 22 percent of U.S.-citizen children had visited emergency rooms within the past year. In contrast, only 13 percent of noncitizen adults and 12 percent of noncitizen children had used emergency room care."

It's also often argued that immigrants are responsible for adding to the crime rate in this country, or that immigrants themselves are dangerous criminals. But this is a myth. In fact, in places where higher concentrations of immigrants live, there is generally less crime.

Why is there less crime in these areas? Immigrants—and undocumented immigrants especially—make an effort to avoid any sort of legal situation that might affect their standing in the United States. A sad consequence of this is that they will even let abuses or crimes committed against them go unreported so as not to call authorities' attention to themselves. If they are given the means to become legal citizens, it may actually result in lower crime rates, as an entire segment of the population would be empowered to report crimes against themselves and others.

In September of 2008, the Immigration Policy Center (IPC) published a report entitled *From Anecdotes to Evidence: Setting the Record Straight on Immigrants and Crime*, in which it presents concrete studies and facts refuting the argument that immigrants generate increased levels of crime.

One of their conclusions, based on data from the Department of Justice, is that the crime rate in the United

States is reduced when the population of undocumented immigrants rises during that same period. From 1994 to 2004, the number of undocumented immigrants doubled to nearly 12 million, but the rate of violent crimes in the U.S. fell by 35 percent, and robberies fell 25 percent.[3]

In addition, the IPC report includes data from a study conducted by the Americas Majority Foundation, an avowed conservative organization, which admitted that crime levels were lower in states with higher concentrations of immigrants. From 1999 to 2006, crime rates had dropped 13 percent in the nineteen states with the largest immigrant populations, while the other thirty-one states saw crime drop only 4 percent.[4]

These various studies have reached a consensus conclusion: there is less crime where there are more immigrants. Of course, anyone who commits a crime should suffer the legal consequences, including deportation if it's applicable, but claims that immigrants are causing a rise in crime are simply not supported by evidence.

3. Because increasingly, immigrants will be needed to replace a retiring workforce.

In the coming years, millions of American baby boomers will be retiring. Currently, there are roughly 38 million people over the age of sixty-five in this country. But by 2050, this figure is expected to rise to 88 million.[5] Who is going to support them? Who will pay for their retirement? Who is going to do the work they left behind? Who will the economic future of the country rest on? Immigrants.

The Pew Hispanic Center has calculated that "between 2000 and 2025 the white working-age population will decline by five million as baby boomers retire from the labor force. Working-age Latinos are projected to increase by 18 million (U.S. Census Bureau, 1999). Thus, the vitality of the U.S. workforce increasingly depends on Hispanic educational progress."[6]

The U.S. population is getting younger, and as it does so, we will need Latin American immigrants to replace the retirees and pay for their Social Security benefits. Without immigrants' energetic manpower, the United States will not be able to continue to grow.

Alan Greenspan, former chairman of the Federal Reserve, agrees with this opinion. "The aging of the population is bound to bring with it many changes to our economy," he said before a Senate committee. "Immigration, if we chose to expand it, could prove an even more potent antidote for the slowing growth in the working-age population. . . . Immigration does respond to labor shortages."[7]

The fact is that the U.S. economy is becoming ever more dependent on working immigrants. According to the Urban Institute, at the start of this century, immigrants made up 34 percent of the workforce in the cleaning industry, 23 percent in fishing and agriculture, 21 percent in the manufacturing sector, and 18 percent in the service industries.[8] And those percentages are only going to increase.

Immigrant workers notwithstanding, people in the

United States are facing a serious challenge when it comes to obtaining higher-paying jobs. I understand that in these tough economic times, many will say that the United States does not need more immigrants to compete for jobs and that our first priority should be to find work for the unemployed currently living here. But migration is not like a faucet that can be turned on and off at our discretion. If we respond to the current economic situation by trying to take immigrants out of our workforce, we won't be able to rely on their labor in the future, when we will depend on it. By legalizing undocumented workers we'll be raising the base level of pay and improving benefits and working conditions for everyone. It's extremely important that we don't lose sight of the country's long-term economic objectives and immigrants' importance in achieving those objectives.

The working-age population—those people between the ages of eighteen and seventy-four—is expected to fall from 63 percent to 57 percent by 2050. In other words, workers in the United States will be forced to increase their productivity. There will be fewer people and more jobs to fill. Considering this fact, reducing immigration would be a mistake.

The U.S. doesn't need fewer immigrants; it needs more.

Ben Bernanke, appointed chairman of the Federal Reserve under former president George W. Bush, is well aware of the contributions immigrants make to the growing U.S. economy.

"Increased rates of immigration could raise growth by raising the growth rate of the labor force," he said in testimony before the House Budget Committee in 2007. "However," Bernanke continued, "economists who have looked at the issue have found that even a doubling in the rate of immigration to the United States, from about 1 million to 2 million per year, would not significantly reduce the federal government's fiscal imbalance."[9]

Bernanke's point was clear: even at our current rate of immigration, the outlook for the United States economy is uncertain. So how many immigrants should be admitted into the United States? It's difficult to set an exact figure, but it's safe to say that the number needs to continue increasing in order to keep our economy strong.

According to data from the Department of Homeland Security, 1,052,415 immigrants became legal permanent residents in 2007.[10] And if we add to that the roughly 425,000 who entered the country without documents that same year (according to the Pew Hispanic Center), then we have a total of 1,477,415 foreigners added to the U.S. population.

It must be said that these numbers are estimates, considering that counting undocumented immigrants is clearly an inexact science, and that the majority—59 percent—of people who become legal permanent residents were already living in the United States. But at the very least, these figures give us some idea of how many immi-

grants officially join the U.S. population permanently.
They also offer us a chance to consider the question of
how many immigrants the U.S. should accept every year
in order to guarantee economic growth and fiscal responsibility.

It's not enough to legalize those who are already here.
It's essential that we establish very realistic figures on how
many foreign workers the country will need every year.
Current numbers are simply too low to be able to respond
to the country's future economic needs.

**4. Because the border fence will never effectively
prevent undocumented immigrants from entering
the country.**

The Mexican writer Carlos Fuentes has described the border between Mexico and the United States as a "scar."
This suggests that the border is the product of a wound.
There, on the frontier, centuries of history clash and
harden. It is the site of a collision between a tank and a
subcompact.

We can assume that the United States will continue to
be a superpower for the next two or three decades (even if
challenged by countries like China and India) and that
Mexico will still be developing. Thus, the northern flow of
immigrants from this relatively poor nation to one of the
wealthiest nations is unlikely to slow.

The question is, How do we stop or at least control the
stream of *un*documented immigration? The answer is far
more complex than simply erecting a fence. The infamous

border fence merely offers a false sense of security and control. It doesn't matter how high or how long it is. Undocumented workers—seeking a better life—will find ways to cross.

Taller fencing won't work, because 60 percent of undocumented immigrants enter the U.S. by airplane. They come here with tourist, business, or student visas, and when those visas expire, they remain here without documents.[11]

Longer, wider fencing won't work either. Let's assume for a moment that the U.S. could physically lock down the entire 1,925-mile-long border with Mexico. What about the 12,383-mile-long coastline? Desperation breeds ingenuity, and I believe we would quickly enter the age of the Mexican *balsero*, or boat person, and that immigrants would resort to paddling their way into the country exactly the way Cuban refugees escape to Florida, and that the so-called coyotes would give way to a new generation of human traffickers known as *tiburones*, or sharks.

For the most part these arguments have fallen on deaf ears, especially after the September 29, 2006, Senate vote approving the construction of seven hundred miles of fencing along the U.S.-Mexico border. This bill faced very little opposition. Eighty senators—including both Barack Obama and John McCain—voted in favor of it. Only nineteen opposed the measure. Any intentions of reaching truly meaningful immigration reform have fallen by the wayside. U.S. policy currently stands on force, fences, and raids.

From 1993 to 2003, only ten miles of fencing were built along the U.S.-Mexico border.[12] But in 2006, the government authorized construction of seven hundred miles of fencing in less than two years.

The total cost of the fence is projected to be at least $6 billion. In other words, each mile of fencing will cost $8.5 million. But Congress, being short on funds, initially approved only $1.2 billion.[13]

The construction of this fence generated a great deal of controversy from the very beginning. Then Senate majority leader Bill Frist, a Republican from Tennessee, spoke for many when he said, "Fortifying our borders is an integral component of national security. We can't afford to wait." Others, like Kevin Appleby, director of immigration and refugee policy at the U.S. Conference of Catholic Bishops, disagreed. "This is not a sign of strength and engagement, but a sign of weakness and fear," he said. "And frankly, speaking as an American, it's an embarrassment."

Shortly after the bill passed in the Senate, President Bush signed it into law.

This action seemed to contradict his earlier position on immigration. In an August 15, 2001, speech at the Hispanic Chamber of Commerce in Albuquerque, New Mexico, for instance, Bush stated, "Mexico is a friend of America; Mexico is our neighbor . . . and that is why it's so important for us to tear down our barriers and walls that might separate Mexico from the United States."

Well, the same president who spoke of tearing down

barriers and walls along the border with Mexico ended up ordering their construction. What happened to the former governor of Texas who claimed to understand immigrants so well? What about the presidential candidate who appealed for the Latino vote in 2000 and 2004? What ever became of the president who considered Mexico one of the United States' closest friends?

Immigration reform was never a priority for Bush. He received a high percentage of the Latino vote in not one, but two elections based on promises that were never fulfilled. He failed to confront this issue until very late in his presidency, and, when he finally did address immigration, he had no political capital left in Congress.

Congress and the Bush administration gave the gift of an exorbitantly expensive fence to a number of border cities. Many of these cities were not happy to receive it.

Eagle Pass and Del Rio, Texas, are two such towns, located along the Mexican border.

"The way to protect the border is not with the wall," Del Rio mayor Efrain Valdez told me during a 2007 interview. "[The undocumented immigrant] is going to take maybe three minutes longer to cross, but he will cross anyway."

Three more minutes. That's all. The undocumented immigrants will cross no matter what—with tunnels, with ladders, smuggled in vehicles, swimming, climbing, jumping, and running.

"The wall will give a false impression of security," Chad Foster, the mayor of Eagle Pass, told me. "Why build a wall when the Rio Bravo already acts as a natural dividing line?"

Since 1848, the Rio Bravo (or the Rio Grande, as it is called in the United States) has effectively served as a 1,254-mile-long separation between Mexico and the state of Texas. As Mayor Foster points out, there is electronic monitoring of the border in addition to the local sheriff's office, the Texas National Guard, and ICE agents who are patrolling the border too. "What we are asking for is more technology to protect the Texas border. Not a wall," Foster says.

It's important to note that Mayors Valdez and Foster— along with many other Texas mayors—are not calling for an open border. Quite the contrary. But they do not believe that a simple fence is going to stop the flow of undocumented immigrants. The fence is a physical response to an economic problem. It is an empty symbolic gesture that does nothing to address a real and complex problem. As long as there are hunger and poverty in Latin America, and as long as there are food, work, education, and opportunity in the United States, the flow of undocumented immigration will continue.

Not only does the fence do little to deter undocumented immigrants (at most, it slows them down or diverts them toward other, more dangerous paths), there is another important consideration: water.

"That worries us," Valdez said, "because the wall is going to cut us off from using the Rio Grande; it is going to deprive us of water." Ninety-five percent of Texas land adjacent to Mexico is privately held. And the ranchers who work that land depend on the river to irrigate their crops and water their livestock.

A fence between Texas and Mexico negatively affects commerce, the environment, water distribution, and the physical border itself, and—most ironically—it fails in its stated purpose of stopping the flow of undocumented immigrants.

It takes them only three extra minutes to cross. Three.

By the end of his second term in office, President Bush had increased the Border Patrol's manpower by eighteen thousand.[14] Interestingly enough, 52 percent of all agents are of Hispanic origin.[15] At the same time, only five hundred miles of fencing had been completed; funds ran out before the other two hundred miles were finished. But the immigrants continued to cross. And they continued to die needlessly.

The fence only delays undocumented immigrants from crossing the border; it doesn't stop them. Many simply find a part of the border where the fence has yet to be built. Why contend with a fence when you can just walk into American territory simply by traveling a little farther? It's that easy, but it's also very dangerous. To get around the fence, immigrants are forced to take increasingly perilous routes through the desert, far from towns and cities, risking dehydration, starvation, and exposure.

Because of these risks, the use of coyotes has become essential. Very few immigrants would dare to attempt a crossing alone. And the cost of hiring a coyote has been rising exponentially. The new fence has been a huge boon for coyotes. These days the fee for an escort to ferry one undocumented worker across the border from Mexico is around two thousand dollars (at a minimum). And if we're talking Central or South America, that price can rise to five thousand dollars or more. Rather than saving the United States any money, the fence has been a huge expense that feeds only the black-market economy.

As New Mexico governor Bill Richardson said during a presidential debate, "I believe if you build a twelve-foot fence you'll get an awful lot of thirteen-foot ladders."

In 2006, the year the construction of the fence was approved, 432 immigrants died while trying desperately to cross the border from Mexico. In 2007, after construction of the fence had begun, 398 deaths were reported. And by the end of the 2008 fiscal year, with five hundred miles of fencing already in place, billions of dollars spent, and hundreds of thousands of undocumented immigrants crossing the border, there were still 386 dead bodies at the border.[16] Even the staunchest opponents of immigration must be appalled that human beings are dying simply because they are looking for a better life. We must find a solution to the problem that is humane and effective; addressing the economic issues that encourage people to leave their home countries would be an excellent start.

We can only conclude that the new fence neither

impedes undocumented immigration—425,000 immigrants continue to cross every year—nor significantly reduces the number of deaths along the border.

In order to achieve a realistic immigration policy in the United States, we need the cooperation of both nations working toward creating a system to legalize those who have recently arrived, and a long-term program to strengthen the economy of developing countries so that their workers won't have the incentive to migrate to the United States.

5. Because it's important that the children of undocumented adults have access to a solid education.

We all suffer when an undocumented student, who was able to receive a primary and secondary education, is prevented from going on to college. A bright young mind is held back from achieving his or her full potential, and the United States loses the benefit of having one more creative, hardworking, well-educated asset to society. We lose the benefit of everything this student could have contributed to medicine or technology, or any number of fields. We potentially gain the responsibility of needing to provide this person, who is virtually guaranteed not to be able to earn a decent wage, with social services.

Each and every year, some 65 thousand undocumented students graduate from high school and are unable to continue on to college.[17] This is a veritable tragedy. It stunts the growth of the students and stunts the U.S. economy.

I've had the opportunity to meet many students who

were brought to the United States as infants and who now find themselves with few options when it comes to life after high school. For instance, there is Marie, whom I interviewed for a television program. Her parents, both undocumented, brought her to the United States when she was barely five years old. She was taking classes at a community college in Missouri when she was threatened with deportation.

Like all the children whom I've interviewed on this topic, she identifies herself as American first and foremost, regardless of where she was born. She has lived most of her life in this country.

"I just want the opportunity to one day become an American citizen and continue my education in law school," she told me. "To me, the United States is my home, and it will continue to be my home even if I have to leave."

Ernesto, a young undocumented Mexican immigrant who lives in California, tells a similar story.

"I was eight years old when they brought me here from Mexico," he said. "We lived with my mother and my two brothers in order to reunite with my sisters, who were living in Long Beach."

Far from being a burden, Ernesto is convinced that young people such as himself—those who have graduated from high school and want to go on to college despite their immigration status—have something to offer this country. "I would say that the United States—California and all the other states—are benefiting from our work and our talent."

Tuition at colleges and universities in the United States is extremely expensive for legal citizens, but the cost is significantly greater for foreign students. These young people can't legally work in the United States, and because most have grown up here and consider it home, returning to their country of birth is not a viable option. In many cases, they don't even speak Spanish very well.

Currently, there is no mechanism in place that permits young students to legalize their immigration status. They were brought into this country by their parents, who undoubtedly felt this was a last resort for their child. They did not make the decision to come here, and they're not responsible for breaking immigration laws. Nonetheless, they are forced to bear the consequences of their parents' actions.

In the past decade, a number of proposals have been brought before Congress to address the predicament facing these young people. All of them have failed.

The House and Senate first addressed this problem in 2001 with what has come to be known as the Development, Relief, and Education for Alien Minors (or DREAM) Act.

The DREAM Act would grant six-year temporary resident status to all students who arrived in the United States before their sixteenth birthday, who have spent at least five years in the country, who demonstrate good moral character, and who have a high school diploma or GED. Students who complete a two-year college diploma or enlist in two years of military service would then gain permanent residency and eventually citizenship. This plan offers a clear reward for effort and dedication.

The last time the Senate debated this proposal was in 2007. But on October 24 of that year, it failed to get the fifty-two out of seventy votes needed for approval. Those opposing the DREAM Act argued that it would encourage undocumented immigration and that it would give local undocumented students an unfair advantage over out-of-state students in terms of admission to state universities by enabling them to pay in-state tuition rates.

True, the DREAM Act would prevent public universities from charging higher tuition to undocumented students than to other state residents. But rather than giving them an advantage over any other applicant, the DREAM Act simply ensures that young undocumented students have the same opportunities that everyone else in this country has.

It merely levels the playing field. Nothing more. Nothing less.

When these students are unable to continue their education beyond high school, they are far more likely to resort to joining a gang or to get stuck in an unsanctioned, low-paying job. It's a real calamity that so many young people are condemned to barely eking out an existence in a country with so much to offer. We must remember that these sixty-five thousand students who miss out on the opportunity to earn a degree every year are innocent victims of circumstance who are extremely motivated to succeed and fulfill their parents' dreams for them. And the United States loses their enormous untapped potential.

Of the many controversial issues surrounding undocumented immigrants, the question of giving their children access to higher education is relatively easy to address.

So the question remains: Why has nothing been done about this?

The historic generosity of the United States can and should be extended toward the youngest and most vulnerable immigrants before anything else—especially because these students are not at all to blame for their legal status and they have so much to offer the country.

6. Because immigration is an economic problem that requires an economic solution.

The phenomenon of immigration is a simple equation. When poverty and joblessness are prevalent in one place, the people who live there naturally migrate somewhere with more opportunities. It's a question of supply and demand. As long as workers in developing countries can earn only five dollars per day and employers in the United States are offering that same amount for thirty minutes to an hour of work, people will continue migrating to the U.S. This we cannot change.

But there are some significant changes that we can make. In the short term, we can restructure the way in which immigrants enter the United States. If we implement a system that protects and integrates them upon their arrival, there will be no incentive for people to enter without documents. In the long term, we need to work with developing countries to help them improve their economies and living standards. Increasing financial independence globally will not only benefit the U.S. by decreasing undocumented immigration, it will boost our own economy and increase trade.

It's easy to overlook the fact that immigration is an act of enormous courage and ambition. It takes an incredible amount of fortitude and bravery to leave your home, your family, and your friends to risk your life in an unknown land. Very few people become immigrants because it's their preference. The vast majority of those who turn to immigration do so out of necessity, as a last resort. In the process, they must make immense sacrifices.

The streets of New York and Chicago are hell in the winter. The cold wind rips at your skin. No matter how much you bundle up in layers of clothing, a heavy coat, scarf, boots, cap, and gloves, the icy wind burns your nose, freezes your jaw, and stabs at your eyes.

And yet these streets are filled with immigrants who for the most part are accustomed to much warmer climates: the taxi driver from India, the bricklayer from Mexico, the bike messenger from Cuba, the parking attendant from the Philippines, and the sidewalk vendor from Colombia, to name just a few. Every one of them has someone or something dear to them that they miss: a parent, a friend, a home, a little beach, a mountain, even the street corner they left behind. And no one can argue that the weather in Chicago is preferable to the tropical climates of their home countries.

So what are they doing here? Why don't they go back to where they came from?

First, there's the obvious answer: the cost of the ticket.

Second, and more important—the reason that they gave up so much to come here in the first place—work is available here, and there is none back home. With the amount of money they can make in this country they are able to support themselves (barely) and still send enough home for two or three families. It is this—and only this—that makes the crossing, the solitude, the frigid winters, and the unbearable heat of the summers worth it.

In the United States, there is a very direct line between labor and the fruits of that labor. If you work hard, generally you'll succeed. This is not an idealized notion of this country. It's a reality. I've seen Latin American farmhands come to the United States, work hard, and save enough to buy their own homes. I've seen street vendors and trash collectors become millionaires.

On the other hand, I know many people who work far more than eight hours a day in San Salvador, Guatemala, Oaxaca, and Medellín and ultimately die in abject poverty. In these places hard work yields minimal results.

What can a young man from Chiapas or Veracruz,

about to graduate from high school or college, envision for his future? The Mexican government simply cannot create enough jobs to accommodate him and the 1.3 million other young people entering the workforce every year in that country.

The increasing polarization of classes that we complain about in the United States is very minor compared to the class differences in developing countries. Latin America is a perfect example of this dichotomy.

A horrible economic disparity has allowed the wealthiest 10 percent of the population to control half of the overall economy. The rich get richer and the poor become destitute. Latin America is still the land of monopolies and oligarchies, a land of the privileged few who break bread among themselves. And as long as everyone there does not have equal opportunities, people will continue to flock to the north. The hardest-working, most determined citizens are Latin America's largest export.

Latin American youth are frustrated by the knowledge that the countries of their birth still contain racial and class barriers that not even the best education can overcome. There is no Obama there. Mexico had Benito Juárez, the first full-blooded indigenous national to become that country's president. He also was a progressive reformer and a symbol of equality. But that was in the late 1800s, and no one has taken his place in the meantime.

I don't know many people at all who return to countries with such limitations. Why would they? I doubt if even Cuban exiles would return to their island if Fidel and Raúl

Castro were to die or otherwise fall from power. Some years ago, the Cuban writer and columnist Carlos Alberto Montaner told me that he didn't think even 5 percent of Cuban exiles would return to a democratic Cuba. And as far as I know, he hasn't changed his position. Those who immigrate to the United States consider it their new home. They love this country and they truly appreciate what it has to offer.

It's only natural that people want to live in an established society, rather than one that is still in the process of being built. University of Miami professor Jaime Suchlicki proposed this concept during a recent conversation that we had about the possibility of a massive Cuban exodus from the island after the rumored (but, as we now know, untrue) death of their dictator, Fidel Castro.

Who would want to wait five or ten years for the end of the blackouts, for a free press and the arrival of supermarkets and modern technology for everyone?

The immigrants working in New York, Chicago, Los Angeles, Houston, and Charlotte aren't about to wait any longer for their countries to improve either. They don't believe in the politicians who promise a government based on trust rather than corruption. They no longer have the patience to wait for better teachers in the public schools. They're not willing to risk one of their children being kidnapped by a narcotrafficker, or having one of their bimonthly paychecks taken from them at gunpoint. They don't buy the propaganda that's broadcast on television. They're no longer willing to wait for improvements that never come, for opportunities that never arrive. They bet on the present, not on the future.

That's why they leave their birth countries, and that's why they won't go back—even if life is very difficult for them in the United States.

Despite wars, politics, and economic crises, the U.S. is still a place where it's possible to reinvent yourself. I've heard many more success stories than failures from people who have come to this country with nothing but a dream. And it's success on the most basic level: a safe place to live, a decent job, education for their kids, and quality health care. In the cities where these immigrants settle, not only do they adapt to American culture, they enhance these places with the flavor of their homeland's culture. What would New York City be without Chinatown, Little Italy, and Spanish Harlem? A much less vibrant place.

This has been my experience. I came here for one year, and just like that, it's become twenty-five.

7. Because it is the best way to help developing countries.

Leaving one's homeland is one of the most difficult decisions a human being can make. Nobody wants to leave family and friends behind or say good-bye to the place where he or she grew up, a place laden with history, emotion, and memory. In many ways, we carry with us all our lives something of our homeland.

What drives people from their native countries? Above all, it's a lack of high-paying jobs. But there are other reasons too, such as violence, corruption, persecution, politics, the lack of liberty, and few cultural opportunities.

These people have lost confidence in their future. They no longer believe that tomorrow will be a better day. They no longer believe that their country is moving in the right direction. And they can't afford to wait around to see if things improve. In general, immigrants are people who have lost faith in their own governments and are no longer willing to entrust their future to failed policies.

Let's examine the case of Mexico.

From 1929 through 2000, Mexico was controlled by the Partido Revolucionario Institucional (PRI), the Institutional Revolutionary Party. There was no democracy. Each president selected his successor. There was no freedom of the press, and political dissent and opposition were extremely limited. Despite the promises of the PRI politicians, Mexico never began to flourish. Instead, it endured one crisis after another. Some of these crises were political, such as the student massacres in 1968 and 1971, in which the government violently quelled massive public demonstrations against its oppression. Others were economic: for instance, when the banks had to be nationalized in 1982 and the so-called December Mistake of 1994, which marked the beginning of one of the worst financial disasters in the nation's history. This catastrophe was quite similar to the current economic crisis in the United States.

In 1848, Mexico lost half its territory to the United
States. But the newly defined border didn't change Mexicans' emotional, familial, commercial, and work-related
ties to the land. Mexican immigration into the United
States has always existed. Since the 1970s, it has grown at a
dramatic rate. Two things led to this wave: new U.S.
immigration laws (which eliminated national quotas
and facilitated family reunification) and the perception
that an unending series of PRI administrations would
never be able to lift Mexico out of its state of underdevel-
opment.

While its neighbor to the north was strengthening its
position as an international superpower, Mexico had to
struggle with the serious problems of poverty, corruption,
social inequality, and one of the worst economic dispari-
ties between classes in the world. This was the legacy of
seventy-one years of PRI leadership.

Vicente Fox's victory in the 2000 election generated enormous hope among Mexicans. Finally, on July 2 of that year,
the PRI was out of power, replaced by Fox's Partido Acción
Nacional (PAN), or National Action Party. Finally, Mexico
was a true representative democracy. And with the new-
found political liberties, the people saw the possibility for a
new economic boom as well. *No nos falles*, they said. Don't
fail us now.

In the midst of this atmosphere of euphoria and change

I interviewed Vicente Fox. One day after his historic victory, Fox told me that he was going to make good on his
campaign promise of creating one million new jobs. This
figure matched the number of young people who entered
the workforce every year.

The idea was to keep Mexican workers from leaving the
country by creating enough high-paying jobs to reverse
the flow of immigrants. Ireland set a good example for
Mexico to follow. By providing its citizens with well-
paying jobs and social benefits, its government had managed to convince Irish expats to return home in greater
numbers than workers who were leaving. And if Ireland
could do it, Mexico could too.

But in the end, Fox failed. He couldn't keep his promises. And just like the PRI governments that preceded
him, he wasn't able to create enough jobs for the Mexican
people. Fox, it turned out, was a better candidate than a
president. And millions continued to leave the country
under his administration.

Fox's successor, Felipe Calderón, also a member of
PAN, aimed to succeed where Fox could not. I spoke with
him during his presidential campaign at his headquarters in
Mexico City in April of 2006, just three short months
before the election. I was surprised to find that the forty-
three-year-old bespectacled candidate was fresh and alert,
despite sleeping only four or five hours a night. He came
from a family with a long tradition in politics—his father
founded the National Action Party—and had one thing on
his mind: erasing the lead held by the candidate of the Par-

tido de la Revolución Democrática (Party of the Demo-cratic Revolution), Andrés Manuel López Obrador.

"Yes, that's the competition," he told me. "And the difference between us is very simple: I'm going to be the employment president, and he is going to kill Mexico's busi-nesses."

After his opponent challenged the initial results, several popular demonstrations, and a partial recount, Calderón won this controversial election by the slimmest of mar-gins. But even today, López Obrador insists that the results were fraudulent.

And Calderón, nearly halfway through his six-year term, is still not known as the "employment president." In fact, he has fallen far short of his own campaign promise to create one million jobs per year.

The single largest source of revenue in Mexico is oil. But the world economic crisis in 2008 instigated a fall in the price of that commodity. Mexico, in spite of modest energy reform, refused to allow foreign investment in oil expro-priation, and its national production fell from 3.3 million barrels per day in 2004 to 2.8 million barrels in 2008. As a result of this sharp decline, Mexico now runs the risk of sliding from an oil-exporting nation to an oil-importing nation by 2015, according to a report in *Forbes*.[18]

And hundreds of thousands of Mexicans continue leav-ing the country every year.

✦

During his first years in office, Calderón has been recognized in the news for fighting narcotrafficking and other related crimes more than anything else. And this brings up another reason why so many Mexicans are fleeing: they no longer feel safe in their own country.

Mexico's Human Rights Commission reported that between 2005 and 2008, 48 million people were victims of crime in Mexico. That's the equivalent of 44,000 separate crimes per day. In other words, nearly half of the country's entire population has been the victim of criminal activity in just three years. The commission also reported that between 2001 and 2008 there were 20,000 kidnappings and 10,500 murders linked to narcotrafficking and organized crime. And out of every 100 crimes, 98 went unpunished.[19]

As a result of these frightening statistics, some 12 million native-born Mexicans have decided to make the United States their new home. And six out of seven Mexicans in the U.S. send money to their families back in Mexico.[20]

After oil, remittances are Mexico's second-largest source of foreign currency. In 2008, Mexicans living in the United States sent $23.5 billion back to Mexico.[21] Although this reflects a slight decrease from the previous year (a 2 percent reduction attributed largely to the economic downturn and the increase in anti-immigrant measures), it is an important source of income, and thousands of Mexican families depend on it for survival. All you have to do is take a quick trip through states like Guanajuato, Michoacán, or Oaxaca to see how entire populations depend on remittances sent from the United States. The United States benefits from this as well, because we get diligent, hardworking laborers; any improvement to Mexico's economy is good for our country too.

It's important to bear in mind two fundamental issues in order to understand this phenomenon.

First, these families generally receive money from relatives in the United States once or twice a month. They use it for basic household expenses, and when there's a bit extra, it goes to pay for school, home improvements, a satellite dish, or a new car, and—in the best-case scenario—to open a small business.

These remittances have the same effect as the microcredit loans that have become so successful throughout the world. They're small amounts of money that can have an enormous impact on individual families, communities, and local economies. It's easy to tell who is receiving these remittances and who isn't, especially in the smaller, more remote towns such as Guadalajara or Monterrey. In the space of a single block, you can see homes that are well kept, have a fresh coat of paint and a satellite dish, and homes that clearly fell into a state of disrepair years ago. Without these remittances, thousands of Mexicans would be living well below the poverty line.

The second fact about remittances is that there are very few men still living in the areas benefiting from this money. And, more recently, there are fewer women as well.

For decades, it was the men who went north, leaving their wives and families at home in Mexico. Immigration is cyclical: you go to the United States during planting or harvesting seasons (or whenever the demand for labor is high), and you come back to Mexico for Christmas and the New Year.

But this cycle of coming and going became more complicated after the Immigration Reform and Control Act, signed November 6, 1986. This bill made it a crime for businesses and individuals to knowingly employ undocumented immigrants, and granted proper documents to those who had been living the United States continuously since 1982.

Crossing from one side of the border to the other wasn't so easy anymore. The measures implemented to make it more difficult for undocumented immigrants to enter the United States have had an unintended consequence. They've made it more likely that those who do make it across will stay longer and may attempt to bring entire families for permanent residence rather than just the man of the house for seasonal work.

A journey that was gradually growing more complicated became a true odyssey after the terrorist attacks of September 11, 2001.

It's of the utmost importance to remember: the nineteen terrorists who hijacked planes and killed nearly three thousand Americans in New York, Washington, and Pennsylvania had nothing whatsoever to do with the millions of immigrants living peacefully within the United States. Unfortunately, one of the many side effects of this tragedy has been a new wave of xenophobia that swept across the nation immediately following this event. Although this fear is understandable, we must not let fear affect the way we treat innocent people, the invisibles who were also killed and who mourned silently along with the rest of the country in the wake of this terrible tragedy.

The history of Mexican immigration is echoed, with certain unique distinctions, in the stories of those coming from other countries around the world.

The 2.5 million Salvadorans who live in the United States sent roughly $3.7 billion back to their families in 2007.[22] But in 2008, thanks in part to the tough economic climate, the remittances were down slightly.

Guatemalans living in the United States sent just over $4.1 million back home in 2007, and sent slightly less in 2008.[23] The same can be said about Hondurans, Colombians, and Dominicans.

Remittances constitute a significant percentage of the gross domestic product for these Latin American countries, and represent the most direct, effective, and safest form of aid coming from the United States. This money is not charity; rather it is an investment in the labor from these countries. This is the basis of our capitalist system, and the United States can only benefit from increasing our ability to produce goods and services, while simultaneously making it possible for developing countries to afford to buy them. If the United States truly wants to aid developing countries and help restore the global economy, its first step should be legalizing the immigrant workers already living here.

In the end, creating and implementing a long-term program of investment in developing countries is essential to slowing the influx of immigrants to the United States. But that will take decades.

In the meantime, allowing the undocumented workers already in the United States to legalize their status is the best way to help millions of poor families. This will free them from the economic apartheid they currently live under and allow them to obtain better, higher-paying jobs while promoting development in their countries of birth.

8. Because it will make the United States a safer place.

The first American soldier killed during Operation Iraqi Freedom was born in Guatemala. The twenty-two-year-old marine, José Antonio Gutiérrez, died on March 21, 2003, near the southern city of Umm Qasr.

Lance Corporal José Antonio Gutiérrez, of the 2nd Battalion, 1st Marine Regiment, 1st Marine Division out of Camp Pendleton, California, was orphaned in Guatemala and grew up on the streets. As a young man he came to the United States to fulfill his dream of becoming an architect. Because he looked young for his age, he was able to attend high school and, as a minor, he was able to get a green card. This immigrant, who gave his life for the United States, was not an American citizen.[24]

Like José Antonio, many immigrants have died—and continue to die—in defense of the United States. More than 114,000 foreign-born soldiers were in the U.S. military as of mid-2009, according to the Immigration Policy Center. This represents almost eight percent of the personnel on active duty.

As I've previously stated, the vast majority of undocumented immigrants are neither terrorists nor criminals. And many of them, like Lance Corporal Gutiérrez, would be proud to take up arms in defense of this country . . . given the opportunity. In order to be a member of the United States Armed Forces, one must be a legal resident. Undocumented immigrants cannot serve.

The wars in Iraq and Afghanistan began after the September 11 attacks. It's worth repeating: not one of the nineteen terrorists who hijacked planes and killed nearly three thousand Americans in New York, Washington, and Pennsylvania entered the United States by crossing the border with Mexico. Not a single one. And none of the 9/11 terrorists were Latin American, nor did they receive training in any Latin American country. Not a single one. However, many Latin American immigrants continue to suffer the consequences of those vicious attacks.

We should focus on locating Osama bin Laden, not persecuting Elvira.

I went to Chicago in August of 2007 to meet Elvira Arellano, but I was too late. She had been deported a few days before I arrived. That summer, many Chicago Latinos were still talking about her.

Elvira had become a symbol.

Elvira Arellano is the undocumented Mexican woman who defied an order of deportation for over a year, seeking refuge in a Chicago church by claiming that it was an official sanctuary. This act of resistance received a great deal of publicity and the admiration of many undocumented immigrants across the country.

She was invited to participate in a march supporting the legalization of undocumented workers that was to take place in Los Angeles. Because of Elvira's passionate desire to inspire others in similar circumstances, she left her sanctuary and traveled to L.A. But she didn't make it. She was sent back to Tijuana with little fanfare. Elvira's case is a perfect example of why current immigration laws simply do not work.

Her arrest separated her from her eight-year-old son, Saúl, who is an American citizen, in the same way that thousands of families have been torn apart by the workplace raids that have been occurring more and more frequently across the country.

What was Elvira's crime? Possessing false documents in order to get a job as a cleaning woman at O'Hare Airport. Yes, it's true, she broke the law—but she was doing

honest work, and she didn't take a job away from anybody; this was an occupation that most people would
never consider. She simply wanted to make a better life for
herself and her son. That's all.

Osama bin Laden is an enemy of the United States.
Elvira and millions of other immigrants are not. Nevertheless, they are paying the price for the crimes of bin
Laden and other terrorists through an immigration policy
that does not distinguish between hardworking immigrants and dangerous criminals.

Just days after her arrest and deportation, the proimmi-
grant march took place without her. But her personal
tragedy did not go unnoticed. The theme of the protest
was "*Todos somos Elvira.*" We are all Elvira.

With very few exceptions all of us, or our relations, living in the United States came from another country—and
not so long ago. But a fierce and vocal minority, consumed
with hatred and prejudice, has managed to impose its anti-
immigrant message on a nation that has traditionally
opened its arms to the newly arrived.

It pains me greatly that I didn't get to Chicago in time
to talk with Elvira. But she came up in each and every conversation I had with an immigrant who—like her—
refuses to give in, and who continues to hope for legal
residency in the United States.

Legalization would make it possible to identify and
document nearly every single person living within this
country's borders, and therefore allow the authorities to
focus exclusively on those individuals who pose a true

risk to national security. Legalizing undocumented immigrants would be the single most effective anti-terrorist measure the U.S. government could take. It would free up millions of dollars that could be used by intelligence agencies to seek out and remove the truly dangerous people from the United States.

I cannot repeat this too often: the vast majority of undocumented immigrants in this country are neither criminals nor terrorists. And now is the time to bring them out of the shadows and into the proper light of American law. It is documenting the undocumented, not mass deportation, that would make the United States a much safer place.

9. Because Barack Obama promised it.

I call it Project 279. For real change to take place in the United States, you need 279 people. It's simple political arithmetic: 218 representatives (out of the 435 that make up the House), 60 senators (out of 100), and the president.

All we need to pass meaningful immigration reform is 279 politicians. And of those 279, it appears that at least 2 are already convinced: President Barack Obama and Senator John McCain. With the leadership of both of these men, things could change for millions of undocumented immigrants, while at the same time, the United States would be able to establish control over its borders and reaffirm the principles of equality upon which it was founded.

On May 28, 2008, in Denver, Barack Obama promised me that, during his first year in office, he would present a proposal for immigration reform. Now the time has come for him to make good on his promise.

When I asked him if it would happen during the first one hundred days of his term, he said, "No." But he added, "What I can guarantee is that we will have, in the first year, an immigration bill that I strongly support."[25]

And it seems that Obama has not forgotten his promise. Three days after he took the oath of office, the official White House Web site listed immigration as one of the priorities on his agenda.

Near the top of the page was a quote from a statement Obama made on the Senate floor on May 23, 2007. It read, "The time to fix our broken immigration system is now. . . . We need stronger enforcement on the border and at the workplace. . . . But for reform to work, we also must respond to what pulls people to America. . . . Where we can reunite families, we should. Where we can bring in more foreign-born workers with the skills our economy needs, we should."[26]

President Obama reiterated his commitment to immigration reform in the very near future during his White House press conference on April 29, 2009. "We can't continue with a broken immigration system. It's not good for anybody. It's not good for American workers. It's dangerous for Mexican would-be workers who are trying to cross a dangerous border. It is putting a strain on border communities, who oftentimes have to deal with a host of undocumented workers. And it keeps those undocumented workers in the shadows, which means they can be exploited at the same time as they're depressing U.S. wages."

And the goal of any new immigration reform should be the following: protect the borders, legalize those who are already here, and reform the system overall so as to benefit the country as a whole.

All right, we've got Barack Obama on our side.

And John McCain too.

"I'm the guy who took over the issue of immigration when it wasn't popular to do so," he told me during a September 2008 interview that took place in Colorado Springs.[27]

In that same interview, the Republican senator from Arizona and presidential candidate assured me that he was in favor of "a path to citizenship" for those undocumented immigrants who have committed no crimes, who pay a fee, and who wait for their turn after those seeking to enter the country legally have been heard.

And then he explained to me why no other solution would be possible. "There's not twelve million pairs of handcuffs in America" to arrest and deport all the undocumented immigrants, he said. "These are God's children."

If Barack Obama and John McCain are in agreement on this thorny issue, the rest of the Democrats and Republicans should be encouraged to work together and overcome the monumental challenge of reforming immigration policy.

Toward the end of 2008, Senate Majority Leader Harry Reid was asked if Democratic control of Congress would make it easier to do something about our immigration policy. His answer was blunt. "On immigration, there's been an agreement between Obama and McCain to move forward on that. . . . We'll do that."[28]

In a conversation I had with him in January of 2009, Senator Reid told me that he hoped the debate on immigration reform would reach Congress in September of 2009.[29]

These statements fill millions of people with hope. The issue is on the administration's agenda, there is a certain amount of consensus on what needs to be addressed, and there is even a tentative date set for discussions to begin.

But if all of the above fails, we'll have to fall back on something more basic: President Obama's promise that we will have an immigration bill some time during his first year in office.

And promises are meant to be kept. It's that simple.

10. Because the United States of America is a nation of immigrants.

Now is not the time to turn our backs on a grand tradition that has served this country well. Immigrants formed the United States, and this tradition should be kept alive. At this pivotal moment in history, by legalizing the status of the millions of undocumented immigrants who are already living here, and creating a new system that allows for the safe, legal, and efficient entry of many more, we can pay our respects to our nation's roots.

American citizens who are descended from immigrants often argue that their ancestors fully complied with immigration laws, and that newcomers today should also fulfill the same requirements before being accepted. Well, the reality of the situation is much more ambiguous and complicated than that.

If the restrictions when the ancestors of current American citizens came to the United States were as stringent as they are today, most would not have been able to enter this country. And that's not all. Thousands of American families have benefited from the same sort of immigration reform that is now being denounced.

Under the 1986 bill, nearly three million undocumented workers legalized their immigration status. The majority of these were Mexicans. But Mexicans aren't the only group of people to have benefited from such massive reform.

According to the 1929 Registry Act, for a mere twenty-dollar fee, any "law-abiding aliens who may be in the country under some merely technical irregularity" could register as permanent residents, providing they had lived in the U.S. since 1921 and were of "good moral character."

Between 1925 and 1965, more than two hundred thousand undocumented European immigrants benefited from this type of reform through a process known as "preexamination," whereby an immigrant would voluntarily leave the country before reentering legally with a visa. Seventy-three percent of those who avoided deportation in this way were of German and Italian descent.[30]

I understand that the United States does not currently have the political will to pass another reform bill like the ones of 1929 and 1986. We are in the midst of an economic crisis, and the general attitude of the nation changed significantly after the September 11 attacks.

There are many alternatives that do not rise to the level of such massive reform, but can still resolve the immigration status of millions of people. Again, let's remember that we're not talking about criminals and terrorists here. We're talking about people who have built our homes, harvested our crops, and cared for our children. They deserve our good faith, and they deserve an opportunity. Just one.

Undocumented immigrants could be our greatest allies in these difficult economic times. Few people work with such dedication and expect so little in return. Few people would be as grateful to receive the opportunity to come out of the shadows and live. Few would fight as hard for the betterment and survival of this nation. All they need is a chance. The same chance given to those who came before them.

Four

THE FIRST HISPANIC PRESIDENT OF THE UNITED STATES

Where is the Latino Barack Obama? If there are more Latinos than African Americans in the United States, why isn't the first minority president Hispanic? When will we see a Latino in the White House?

It must be said that the triumph of Barack Obama on November 4, 2008, is an extraordinary event for a nation that spent so many decades bearing the cross of slavery, followed by even more years of racism and discrimination. There can be no doubt that Obama's election represents an unprecedented advance in race relations for a country that was, in many ways, founded by slaves and their owners.

It is also an incontrovertible fact that the United States is well on its way to becoming a majority Latino country. That being the case, the question is no longer *whether* the United States will have a Hispanic president but *when*.

᠅

A few days after the August 28 Democratic National Convention in Denver—when Obama gave his first speech as
his party's official candidate for the presidency—the Census Bureau presented us with a very clear picture of what
the United States is going to look like in the future. And
the eighty thousand people in Mile High Stadium for
Obama's acceptance speech were an unmistakable reflec-
tion of this picture.

Very soon, the United States will cease to be a distinctly
black-and-white nation. There will be miscegenation,
mestizaje, and mixing. We will no longer be able to clearly
define people by race, color, or religion. This country will
be multiethnic, multiracial, multicultural, and multilingual.

According to the *New York Times*, "The census calcu-
lates that by 2042, Americans who identify themselves as
Hispanic, black, Asian, American Indian, Native Hawai-
ian and Pacific Islander will together outnumber non-
Hispanic whites."[1] This report was significant, because
previous calculations had predicted this would not occur
until 2050. In other words, minorities are growing much
more quickly than anticipated.

The Hispanic population will swell from 46.7 million in
2008 (15 percent of the total population) to 132.8 million in
2050 (roughly 30 percent of the total).

Still, I would like to know exactly when Latinos will

become a clear majority in the United States, with over 50 percent of the population. The Census Bureau couldn't help me there.

I spoke with two scientists, and neither one would venture a prediction more than fifty years into the future. And they're right. Many variables are impossible to calculate, from changes in immigration patterns to wars, natural disasters, and terrorist attacks.

Despite all that, I decided to do a little mathematical exercise. And this is what I came up with.

Latinos will become the majority demographic in this country in less than a hundred years. If the variables remain more or less constant, by 2106, there will be more Latinos than non-Hispanic whites in the United States.[2]

This population growth is due largely to two factors: immigration and a high birth rate.

According to projections based on current immigration policies, the Census Bureau data has the number of foreigners coming to the United States rising from 1.3 million per year to over two million by midcentury.[3] The majority of those immigrants will be from Mexico.

Ana Teresa Aranda, a Mexican government undersecretary responsible for population, immigration, and religious affairs, reports that nearly 12 million Mexicans live in the United States. And according to her data, some 580,000 enter the country every year.[4] (Of course, these figures predate the onset of the current U.S. economic crisis.)

But the most interesting part of all this data is that today, at the outset of the twenty-first century, the single greatest contributor to the U.S. Latino population is the number of births in this country, not the number of immigrants arriving.

"In the 1970s, '80s and '90s, there were more Hispanic immigrants than births [among the Latino population]," explained Jeffrey Passel, senior demographer at the Pew Hispanic Center. "This decade, there are more births than immigrants. Almost regardless of what you assume about future immigration, the country will be more Hispanic and Asian."[5]

This is a veritable demographic revolution. More than half the children born in the United States since the turn of the century have been Hispanic. Here are the statistics:

Between April of 2000 and July of 2007, 10.2 million Hispanic babies were born in the United States. During the same time frame, the rest of the non-Hispanic population grew by only ten million. The Latino population as a whole grew 29 percent, compared with 4 percent for the rest of the population.[6]

But let's break it down some more.

Latin American families traditionally have more children than American or European families. This tradition continues when they immigrate to the United States.

The Hispanic population is growing by 3.3 percent per year, while the white population is growing at a rate of only 0.3 percent.[7] This enormous contrast generated headlines like the following from *El nuevo herald*: "Hispanics Save U.S. from Demographic Crisis." The corresponding article begins with the following sentence: "If not for the births of Hispanic children, the United States could face a long-term demographic decline similar to those experienced by Germany, Japan, and other industrialized nations."[8]

Recently, Hispanics became the country's largest minority, surpassing African Americans, and in less than a century they could become a clear majority. Thanks in part to the growth of the Hispanic population, minorities already combine to form a majority in three states—New Mexico, at 58 percent, California, at 57 percent, and Texas, at 52 percent—as well as the District of Columbia, at 68 percent.[9]

This change in population has enormous cultural consequences.

Recently I read an article by the talented young French rapper Diam's, who was born in Cyprus and grew up in a Paris suburb. According to the *International Herald Tribune*, she represents a new generation of French artists of immigrant heritage who are appropriating French culture. "The France of the baguette and the beret is not my France," the then twenty-six-year-old said in an interview with the paper. "I don't relate to that France. It doesn't mean anything to me. I like to eat kebabs. I wear hoods."[10]

Well, the same sort of cultural change that is taking place in France and other countries across Europe is alive and well here in the United States. It's the Hispanic impact. Nobody knows exactly what the final result will be, but one thing we can be sure of is that it will not be pure; it will be a mixture. One can only imagine.

Even today, it's easy to find attitudes like those voiced by Diam's, in France and here in the United States. The country of hot dogs, baseball, and pop music doesn't always mean something to people from other parts of the world. To them, the United States means soccer, tacos, and reggaeton.

More tortillas than bagels are consumed every year in the United States. In Texas and California, José is a more popular name than Michael. According to *USA Today*, on the list of the country's most common surnames, Garcia and Rodriguez are ahead of Brown and Miller. And some of the highest-rated radio and television shows in Miami, Houston, Phoenix, Los Angeles, San Francisco, Chicago, and New York are Spanish-language programs.

By their very presence, Hispanics are promoting everything from the social justice and equality of Cesar Chavez; the music of Shakira, Calle 13, and Fonseca; the voices of Plácido Domingo and the tenor Juan Diego Flórez; the magisterial notes of the pianist Gabriela Montero; and the words of Junot Díaz, Isabel Allende, and Sandra Cisneros, among many others.

It's the Latinization of the United States. This doesn't mean that the United States is going to become a Latin nation. It simply means that the presence and progress of Latinos will be a determining factor in the country's future.

This is precisely the theme of an excellent book entitled *Latinos and the Nation's Future* by former San Antonio mayor and former secretary of Housing and Urban

Development Henry Cisneros. "The Latino population is now so large, its trajectory of growth so rapid, its contrast in relative age to that of the general population so stark, that it will not be possible for the United States to advance without substantial, and so far unimagined, gains in the economic, education, and productive attributes of the nation's Latino community,"[11] writes Cisneros, one of the nation's most influential Hispanics, someone whom many people once thought might become the first Latino president.

Nevertheless, Latinos haven't always played a prominent role in American society, nor, at one time, did they seem likely to. As the Colombian actor and comedian John Leguizamo once joked, "There were no Latin people on *Star Trek*; this was proof that they weren't planning to have us around for the future."[12]

The influence of the growing Latino population on the United States can be seen in what we eat, the styles of our dance, and even in the way that we speak.

The United States is (or is on the verge of becoming) the second-largest Spanish-speaking nation on earth. In 2007, the Census Bureau calculated that 34,547,077 people over the age of five speak Spanish at home. It's impossible to know whether this figure includes all Spanish-speaking undocumented immigrants.

In other words, there may well be more Spanish speakers in the United States today than there are in Argentina, Colombia, or Spain. And if it's not the case yet, it will be soon.

The United States is the only country I know of where the people think it's better to speak one language than two. "The reality is that this is a country that should speak English," said former New York mayor Rudy Giuliani, during his recent, unsuccessful presidential campaign.[13] I would add to that at least one more language.

Barack Obama, on the other hand, emphasized that many Europeans speak multiple languages—"it's embarrassing when Europeans come over here, they all speak English, they speak French, they speak German . . ."—and Americans don't.[14] It's true. In one of his columns, the journalist Andrés Oppenheimer pointed to a Eurobarometer public opinion poll covering the twenty-seven members of the European Union that concluded that 56 percent of Europeans speak at least one language in addition to their native tongue.[15]

During a campaign speech he gave in Georgia, now-president Obama recognized the enormous growth in the Hispanic population and culture, telling the crowd, "You need to make sure that your child can speak Spanish."[16]

The fact of the matter is that Hispanic immigrants are rapidly integrating themselves into the United States, learning English, and earning better salaries and gaining more education.

"We are changing the United States," Harry Pachon, professor of public policy at USC and president of the Tomás Rivera Policy Institute, once told me. "But the United States is also changing us." And he went on to tell me that when he asked a group of Latino parents which language their children watch TV in, seven out of ten said they watched TV in English. It's a generational change, he assured me.

And that lends itself to the view that being bilingual is better.

The Census Bureau estimates that 78 percent of Latinos are bilingual, from those who can speak and write fluently in both Spanish and English to those who have a basic understanding of both languages.

It makes sense. Spanish is the way of maintaining the culture of a departed nation, a way of staying connected to one's roots. English, on the other hand, leads to success in the United States.

There are already a number of bilingual neighborhoods and areas in the United States: Hialeah and Little Havana in Miami; Pilsen in Chicago; East Los Angeles, Pomona and West Covina in California; and large sections of Brooklyn and New Jersey, among hundreds of others.

Spanish is spoken in each and every corner of the United States. In one ABC News/*Good Morning America* poll, 78 percent of Americans said that they often or sometimes come into contact with people who speak mainly Spanish.[17] Even Bill Clinton once said that he would have liked to be the last U.S. president who didn't speak Spanish.

Spanish has assured itself a place in the United States for the foreseeable future for five reasons: the constant influx of millions of Spanish speakers, the proximity of many Hispanic communities to the Mexican border, the use of cell phone and Internet technology for keeping in touch with friends and families in Latin America, the Spanish-language print and broadcast media that reinforce and reaffirm the language's importance, and the historic custom among Hispanics to speak Spanish in the home as a way of staying connected to one's roots.

But despite all of the above, many people continue to resist the idea of the United States as a bilingual nation.

"I don't think it's appropriate for a national figure to declare that children should be learning Spanish," said Mauro Mujica, head of the lobbying group U.S. English, in response to President Obama's suggestion. "In a nation where more than three hundred languages are spoken, English is the unifying one."[18]

But this argument is false. The United States is unified by its values: the idea—established in the Declaration of Independence—that all men are created equal, without regard for their national origin, religion, race, or sex; that it is tolerant of diversity, accepting of immigrants, and constantly looking toward the future in new and innovative ways.

It is these values—not the English language—that make the United States the unique place that it is.

Nevertheless, it occasionally seems like the more Spanish is being spoken, the louder the calls to make English the country's official language. In 2007, a Zogby poll found that 83 percent of Americans were in favor of this.[19]

In fact, the Republican Party platform for the 2008 national convention in Minneapolis took a very clear stance on this issue: "We support English as the official language in our nation."[20]

And Latino voters heard this message loud and clear. Two out of every three Latinos voted against the Republican candidate.

Every time I'm on the road, either on assignment or on a book tour, I meet Hispanic parents who introduce their children to me. But in recent years, I've noticed a very significant change in this ritual.

Before, people usually said things like, "I see you on the news," or, "I read your book." Now I hear, "This is Gustavo; he's going to become the first Hispanic president," or, "This is Alejandra; she's going to be the first Latina in the White House." Gustavo just recently took his first steps. And Alejandra is only two years old.

I'm convinced that the first Hispanic president of the United States of America has already been born.

Some think that Henry Cisneros will be the first. Others think that it will be former New Mexico governor Bill Richardson.

I'm more inclined to think the first Latino president is in elementary school, or perhaps sending text messages from his or her cell phone during a high school Spanish class. He or she will be a mix of Latin American and Anglo-Saxon, a concurrence between the North and the South, a midway point between white and black.

Like Barack Obama, the first Hispanic president will be of mixed race. And that's where his or her strength will radiate from. It's the union of differences that gives birth to originality.

The first Hispanic president won't have to define him- or herself as American or as Latino. He or she will be both, without having to offer excuses or justifications. He or she will carry their history and their roots in the color of their skin and in their last name. He or she will be at once indigenous and European, Latin American and Anglo-Saxon together and indistinguishable.

"The ulterior goals of History," wrote José Vasconcelos in his 1925 book, *The Cosmic Race*, are "to attain the fusion of peoples and cultures." He concluded, prophetically, "The so-called Latin peoples . . . are the ones called upon to consummate this mission."[21]

Barack Obama is a global mixture: a mother from Kansas, a father from Kenya; born in Hawaii, raised in Indonesia; educated at Harvard and molded in Chicago. His history touches upon every continent. A Hispanic president will be equally complex and unique in his or her combination race, color, and origin.

There is an inevitable question that arises: If there are more Latinos than African Americans in the United States, why was it Barack Obama—and not a Cisneros, a Lopez, or a Villaraigosa—who became the nation's first minority president? The answer may lie in the number of candles on a birthday cake.

Hispanics are generally younger than the rest of the

American population. In 2007, the Hispanic population had a median age of 27.6 years, compared with the population as a whole at 36.6 years.[22] In other words, the first Latino president may well be in class right now, watching a movie on his laptop, visiting Mexico with his parents, or simply out playing soccer.

One out of every four Hispanics is under eighteen years old. Barack Obama, at forty-seven years of age, reached the White House first.

During the historic days surrounding Obama's victory, I had the opportunity to sit down with two people who have spent more time studying the progress of Hispanics in the United States than perhaps anyone else. And I asked Raul Izaguirre, former president of the National Council of La Raza and executive director of the Center for Community Development and Civil Rights at Arizona State University, if he thought that—at the age of seventy-nine—he would one day see the first Hispanic president of the United States.

"Yes, I hope so," he told me with absolute conviction. "There are very dedicated people, people who have the capacity to become president. There are people with the intelligence of a Barack Obama. The only thing that is missing is for them to present themselves and to open up a conversation with the American public. They need to have an opportunity through the media to get to know the American people."

Arturo Vargas, the executive director of the National Association of Latino Elected and Appointed Officials, or

NALEO, was a bit more realistic. "We're heading in that direction," he told me. "We've made a lot of progress. But we can't fool ourselves. There's still a lot of work to be done. Because, yes, nearly ten million Latinos voted [in the 2008 presidential election]. But seventeen million could have voted."

The path has been carved out. At some point during the next century, Hispanics will become the majority. But before that takes place, a Latino will be able to stand on the White House lawn and say, *Mi casa es su casa*.

Five

THE LATINO VOTE 2008

On Tuesday, November 4, 2008, 9.7 million Latinos went to the polls.[1] This was an extraordinary increase over the 7.6 million Latinos who voted during the 2004 elections.[2]

Many of the people who took part in the 2006 marches in support of legalization and better treatment for immigrants in general, in cities like Los Angeles and Chicago, became new voters. The chants of "*Hoy marchamos, mañana votamos*"—Today we march, tomorrow we vote—were not a warning, nor were they an announcement. They were a wake-up call to the proverbial sleeping giant.

A number of Latino organizations were successful in three areas: one, converting permanent residents into full-fledged American citizens; two, registering the new citizens to vote; and three, getting them to the polls on November 4.

NALEO reported that one in six Latino voters (15 percent) was voting in his or her first presidential election.

And the turnout levels were extraordinarily high: 92 percent of registered Latino voters showed up on Election Day, compared with 74.69 percent of registered voters overall.[3]

The only negative in this whole process is the fact that there could potentially have been 17 million Latinos—U.S. citizens over the age of eighteen—registered to vote. Instead, there are only 9.7 million. In other words, we're throwing away 7.3 million votes. Although we've made incredible progress, there's still work to be done to ensure that every Latino's voice is heard.

Regardless of the numbers, it was thanks to the Hispanic vote that Barack Obama won states like Florida, Nevada, New Mexico, and Colorado—which had fallen into Republican hands in 2004. Countrywide, Barack Obama garnered 67 percent of the Latino vote versus John McCain's 31 percent.

On a state-by-state breakdown, the numbers went like this: New Jersey, 78 percent; Nevada, 76 percent; California, 74 percent; Illinois, 72 percent; New Mexico, 69 percent; Texas, 63 percent; Colorado, 61 percent; Florida, 57 percent; and Arizona, 56 percent.[4]

There can be no doubt that the Latino vote was a tremendous source of support for Obama, although it was certainly not the only factor that contributed to his broad margin of victory over McCain. In the end, the electoral college count was 365 for Obama versus 173 for McCain.

It's also important to consider the fact that this presidential election took place when the country was in the throes of a terrible economic crisis—the worst since 1929. Equally important were the debilitating approval ratings of the outgoing president (22 percent in January of 2009).[5] Those were the two predominant factors that decided the election.

But minorities did play an essential role. If the only voters in the 2008 election had been non-Hispanic whites, McCain would be the president of the United States. Fifty-five percent of white voters opted for McCain, compared with 43 percent who voted for Obama.[6]

McCain made a good effort to rally, but in the end he fell short. Early polling done in late 2007 showed him with barely 23 percent of the Hispanic vote.[7] He was able to raise that to 31 percent by the election, but that just wasn't enough. Since Ronald Reagan in 1980, every Republican candidate who failed to get a third of the Hispanic vote has lost.

McCain faced a monumental challenge in winning over Hispanic voters. An interview conducted all the way back in 2005 by the Latino Coalition was already forecasting difficulties for Republicans among the Hispanic community.

"There is real danger for a repeat of the Pete Wilson era that alienated Hispanics from the GOP for years," Robert de Posada, president of The Latino Coalition, said. "The Republican leadership in Congress has failed miserably in keeping the coattails of President Bush among Hispanic voters."[8]

Those would prove to be prophetic words.

Florida presents us with an interesting case. The Republicans won the state in 2000 and 2004. Despite that fact, however, the Cuban population is losing its traditional place of power within the Hispanic voting public. In an interview with the *New York Times*, political analyst Sergio Bendixen warned that the percentage of Cuban American voters within the Florida Hispanic community in general had fallen from 75 percent in 2000 to only 45 percent in 2008.[9]

Considering this dramatic demographic shift, by adopting their traditional strategy of focusing their Florida campaign on opposition to the Castro regime in Havana, the Republicans committed a major strategic error. That issue wasn't going to capture the interest of non–Cuban American voters. The importance of the Puerto Rican vote in central Florida is the key to explaining why McCain lost that state. Issues like the economy and the return of American troops from Iraq were much more important to Puerto Ricans than to their *hermanos* from Cuba.

Obama, on the other hand, was faced with a different challenge. He had to disprove those people who suspected that the Latinos who had voted for Hillary Clinton in the primaries would not vote for Obama in the general election. The historic tension between blacks and Hispanics was another campaign question mark. Would Latinos turn out in significant numbers for an African American candidate?

In the end, Obama won in convincing style, in part

because of the $20 million his campaign invested in getting out the Latino vote, and also because he so adeptly voiced his opinions on the real issues that matter to the Hispanic community.

By definition, those Latinos who are registered to vote have already resolved their own immigration status: either they were born in the United States, or they have become full American citizens. So it's no surprise that two-thirds of Latino voters (67 percent) told NALEO interviewers that the issue concerning them most was the economic situation.

However, an impressive 73 percent said that they were in favor of some type of immigration reform that would legalize the status of the millions of undocumented immigrants.[10]

The immigration issue was not at the top of the list for most Latino voters (according to the NALEO survey, a mere 6 percent considered it the most important issue of 2008), but there was enormous symbolic weight that came with knowing that a candidate was reaching out and listening to Hispanics. In other words, a candidate's position on immigration and legalization was just one way for Latinos to know who was their friend and who wasn't.

The New Rule

A new rule of today's American politics is that nobody can make it to the White House without the Latino vote and without reaching out to Latino voters via the Spanish-language media. Nobody.

I still remember back in 1984 and 1985, when I was a television reporter in Los Angeles; virtually no politicians spoke Spanish or were remotely interested in giving interviews to Channel 34, the only station that broadcast in Spanish in those days. Occasionally the non-Latino politicians had an assistant or two who spoke Spanish. Or worse, they would say, half jokingly, that their driver or gardener was fluent. Either way, they didn't take us seriously.

Today things are radically different.

In Southern California, no politician can hope to be elected to local office without getting some exposure on the dozen or so channels that broadcast locally in Spanish. Speaking Spanish isn't a requirement, but it helps. And the reason is simple: Spanish-language broadcasts are the most watched programs in Los Angeles.

We mustn't underestimate the importance of being bilingual; it led to Antonio Villaraigosa's election as the mayor of Los Angeles on May 17, 2005. He was the city's first Latino mayor in 133 years. His Hispanic predecessor, Cristobal Aguilar, left office in 1872.

Los Angeles has been Latinized. The Census Bureau reported that in 2000, forty-six of every one hundred residents were Hispanic. Today, more than half the children born in the county have Latino surnames.

After a very controversial billboard promoting a local Spanish-language television station was erected along the 605 freeway, the city is occasionally referred to as "Los

Angeles, Mexico." Los Angeles—or, to be more exact, El
Pueblo de Nuestra Señora la Reina de los Ángeles Porciún-
cula, as it was named by a Spanish explorer in 1769—was
originally part of northern Mexico. After the 1848 Mexican
American War, it was forcibly converted into one of the
most diverse, vigorous, and creative communities in the
United States.

Today, Los Angeles is a benchmark for this country's
future. It is, without a doubt, one of the most multicultural
cities in the world, and—with a majority-Hispanic population—it offers us a glimpse of what the United States
will look like at the end of the twenty-first century, and the
kind of political influence Latinos will wield.

Antonio Villaraigosa was one of the few politicians
called to an emergency meeting by Barack Obama in late
2008 to work on solutions to the economic crisis. He
hadn't taken the oath of office yet, but Obama understood
that he would need the support of Villaraigosa and the rest
of the Hispanic population in order to govern effectively.

What first occurred in Los Angeles has now begun to
permeate the rest of the country as well. It will be a matter
of course that future Republican and Democratic political
candidates seek out the Latino vote through Spanish-
language media.

The Debates

For the first time in history, most of the early presidential
candidates from both parties participated in two forums

organized by Univision and broadcast nationwide in
Spanish.

The format was complicated, and there were a number
of technical obstacles to overcome. The candidates would
speak English, and their words were simultaneously translated into Spanish. My coanchor on Noticiero Univision,
María Elena Salinas, and I asked the questions in Spanish,
and the candidates—using a small earpiece—were able to
hear them in English. Ultimately, this system worked to
perfection.

New Mexico governor Bill Richardson, the first Hispanic candidate in the history of the Democratic Party,
wanted to speak in Spanish for this groundbreaking
debate. Senator Chris Dodd, who learned Spanish during
his time with the Peace Corps in the Dominican Republic,
was also ready to do so. But the other candidates—
Senator Hillary Clinton, Senator Joseph Biden, Senator
Barack Obama, former senators John Edwards and Mike
Gravel, and Congressman Dennis Kucinich—felt this
would put them at a disadvantage and agreed to participate only if everyone spoke only in English before having
their words translated into Spanish.

And that was how it went. All the candidates agreed to
the rules of the game, and in the end the only one who
didn't attend was Senator Biden, because of a scheduling
conflict with a pending trip to Iraq.

The debate took place at the University of Miami on
September 9, 2007, and it was the story of the day. Hundreds of journalists from all over the world were on hand
to cover the event.

And every once in a while, during a brief moment between questions, I found myself thinking that what we were witnessing that Sunday night was a radical shift in the United States. Everyone at this event was either speaking Spanish or being translated into Spanish.

Without a doubt, Spanish is rapidly becoming America's second national language. Most of the major-party candidates for the 2008 election employed people among their campaign staff who specialized in promoting their candidate through Spanish-language media.

I haven't forgotten that George W. Bush reached the White House with a few words of broken Spanish: "*Yo puedo hablar español más bueno que ellos,*" he said in 2000, referring to the Democrats and their candidate, Al Gore— "I can speak Spanish more good than they can." And he was right. Gore was able to say only, "*Sí, se puede.*" Yes, we can. But in the end, Gore simply could not.

Bush courted Hispanic voters in Spanish, in Spanglish, and in words that were sometimes unintelligible in Spanish or English. But it worked: he won 34 percent of the Latino vote in 2000 and a surprising 44 percent in 2004. Both times it was enough to get him to the White House.

Certainly, the Hispanic voters who went to the polls in 2008 wanted much more than a few words in Spanish. What Bush had done eight years before was no longer enough.

But the charm hasn't worn off completely. Trying to

speak Spanish (or allowing him- or herself to be translated) during a nationally televised event expresses a politician's interest in, and respect for, Hispanic culture. It's that simple. And that's why the presidential candidates agreed to participate in this form of debate during the primaries.

As the Cuban American businessman José Cancela says, "We want to be courted in the language we make love in."[11] In other words, that's Spanish.

But it's also a question of identity. Even those who can't speak or understand the language well can usually toss out a few Spanish phrases—"*¿Cómo estás?*", "*Pásalo bien*," or the standard "*Buenos días*"—to let other Hispanics know that they're part of the same group. It's a code.

The seven Democratic candidates who participated in that Spanish-language forum took a calculated political risk. There are some voters who believe that English should be the only language spoken in this country, and that appearing on a Spanish-language news program sows the seeds of division.

But for the first time in history, seven candidates appeared in a presidential debate and spoke directly to Hispanic voters in their own preferred language . . . and the world didn't come to an end.

It took the Republicans a little longer, but in the end, they came to the same conclusion as their Democratic counterparts and agreed to participate in the same form of debate. The benefits of doing so far outweighed the risks of alienating some of their core voters.

The Republican event also took place at the University

of Miami, on December 9, 2007, in the midst of a palpable anti-immigrant climate. Osama bin Laden had not been captured. But when it came to Elvira Arellano, who had sought refuge in a Chicago church, yes, she had been arrested, charged, and deported to Mexico.

to see who would come across as the most anti-immigrant. This competition was won hands down by Congressman Tom Tancredo, the only Republican candidate who chose not to participate in the Univision-sponsored debate. He refused to be translated into Spanish.

However, all the others accepted the nation's changing reality. And this new reality is reflected in a Census Bureau report.

In late 2007, the United States had 858,289 people named Garcia, 804,240 named Rodriguez, and 775,072 named Martinez—more than the number of Andersons, Taylors, or Thomases.

The Hernandezes (706,372) outnumber the Moores, Thompsons, and Whites. There are more Lopezes (621,536) than Lees and more Gonzalezes than Harrises and Clarks.[12]

I believe numbers like these are the reason why former New York mayor Rudy Giuliani, former Arkansas governor Mike Huckabee, Congressman Duncan Hunter, Senator John McCain, Congressman Ron Paul, former Massachusetts governor Mitt Romney, and former senator Fred Thompson decided to attend the debate.

The conclusion is unmistakable: during a general

election, failing to seek out Hispanic votes equals political suicide.

The Republicans face the additional challenge of overcoming the fact that Democrats have historically dominated the Latino vote. Add to this the perception that Republicans were in part responsible for the failure of immigration reform, and their challenge may be insurmountable.

A close and careful analysis of the Republican candidates' stance on immigration clearly illustrates that they did not support comprehensive reform. It also shows that—before there could be any talk about legalizing the 12 million undocumented immigrants in the United States—they wanted to secure the border. These positions clashed with the findings of a number of surveys indicating that the majority of Hispanic voters support the legalization of immigrants.

With the exception of John McCain, none of the Republican candidates could come up with a satisfactory resolution to this conflict. The immigration reforms proposed by the Republicans were quite different from those that George W. Bush had defended eight years before.

During his campaign, Bush tried to woo Hispanics by speaking Spanish, promising to treat immigrants with compassion, saying that he would be Mexico's best friend, and maintaining a hard line against Cuba.

But above all, he recognized that the values of many Hispanic voters coincided with the Republicans' conservative agenda. Bush and his political adviser Karl Rove calculated that Republicans and Hispanics could walk hand in hand when it came to the issues of family, abortion, and religion.

The former Texas governor may not have seen everything clearly with regard to Iraq or the economy, but when it came to courting Hispanic voters, he definitely knew what to do.

The Republicans need Hispanics if they want to return to the White House. They have to re-create Bush's victories in Florida, Colorado, New Mexico, and Nevada. And the courtship began with that debate. Ultimately, that presidential debate illustrated that Hispanics had reached what Henry Cisneros calls a "critical mass."

The Republican candidates realized that they could not win the White House without the votes of the Garcias, the Rodriguezes, and the Martinezes. And they recognized that we are experiencing one of the greatest political changes in this country's history.

In addition to these two debates, I also had the opportunity to attend a debate, cosponsored by CNN and Univision and hosted by the University of Texas–Austin, between Barack Obama and Hillary Clinton. I was joined by fellow journalist John King and moderator Campbell Brown. (Not long after the debate, the three of us would be parodied—quite humorously, I must admit—on *Saturday Night Live*.)

The debate, which took place on February 21, 2008, was one of Senator Clinton's last chances to derail Obama's momentum leading up to the Texas primary.

Much of the debate was focused on their differing proposals for health care, immigration, and the war in Iraq.
But more than anything, interest focused on whether
Hillary could hand Obama a convincing defeat and dispel
the aura of invincibility that was forming around him.

No matter which of the two candidates became the
Democratic nominee, history was being made. For the
first time, either a woman or an African American would
be vying for the White House. And with a war in Iraq and
an increasingly unpopular Republican president leaving
office, the Democratic candidate would have a very real
chance at winning.

During this debate, Senator Clinton tried to paint Senator Obama as a gifted orator who lacked experience. "I do
think that words are important and words matter," she
said. "But actions speak louder than words."[13]

Obama countered by explaining his strongest positions—particularly his unequivocal rejection of the war in
Iraq—and then proceeded to dismiss Clinton's notion
that his campaign promises were all talk, stating that it was
ridiculous to suggest that his supporters "are being duped.
The implication is that the people who have been voting
for me or involved in my campaign are somehow delu-
sional."[14]

As the ninety-minute debate came to an end, there was
no clear winner. And that outcome favored Obama. From
that night on, nobody and nothing were able to stop him.

Hillary Clinton waited until the summer before admitting defeat, and there was enormous pressure for Obama

to select her as his vice presidential running mate. But Obama formed a commission to research the matter, and in the end, it was Delaware senator Joseph Biden whom he chose. Hillary Clinton's name would come up later, as Obama's choice for secretary of state.

After he was officially declared the Democratic candidate for the presidency, some doubts began to surface about whether the Hispanics who were so loyal to Clinton in the primaries would turn out in support of Obama at the polls in November. Hillary had garnered more Latino votes than Obama, and old theories about tensions between the Hispanic and African American communities resurfaced.

Many commentators asked, "Would Hispanics vote for an African American candidate?"

Any doubt vanished like a puff of smoke in the general election. Hillary's Latino supporters sided solidly with Obama; nearly seven out of ten voted for him.

Hispanics and the Future of Politics

In the 2008 elections, the Democratic Party recovered the majority of Latino supporters that had been lost to the Republicans in 2004.

The results show that Hispanic voters felt more closely aligned with the Democrats on essential issues like the war and the economy. And on the supremely important issue of undocumented immigration, the majority of Latino voters believe that the Democratic Party will fight harder for reform than the Republicans will.

And of course we can't discount the Obama factor. It's been generations since the United States has had such a young, charismatic, and dynamic speaker and political leader as Barack Obama. He was, after all, a writer before he became president. And Hispanics, like millions of voters representing other ethnic groups, responded to his message of hope and change.

The Democrats went from earning 53 percent of the Latino vote in 2004 to 67 percent in 2008. On the other hand, the Republicans fell from carrying 44 percent of Latinos in 2004 to 31 percent in 2008; that was the exact same percentage they managed in the 2000 election. Eight years of the strides that Republicans had made toward courting Hispanic voters evaporated in one single election.

The *Wall Street Journal*'s editorial board concluded, "The demographic reality is that the GOP can't win national elections while losing such a large share of the fastest-growing ethnic minority in the country."[15]

Republican Senate Minority Leader Mitch McConnell gave a speech in which he proposed a new strategy for winning more Hispanic votes in the future: "Polling suggests that Hispanic voters are even more conservative on a number of issues than the average American," he said. "About half say that tax cuts are the best route to economic growth. Nearly eighty percent oppose abortion. As Reagan put it, 'Hispanic voters are Republicans. They just don't know it yet.'"[16]

If the Republicans are not able to significantly increase their support among Hispanics—and if states like Arizona and Texas begin to vote Democratic—then they will be looking at the future through blue-tinted glasses.

"The GOP won't be a majority if it cedes the young or Hispanics to Democrats," former Bush adviser Karl Rove wrote in *Newsweek* shortly before John McCain's defeat. It was Rove's strategy that enabled Bush to win nearly half the Hispanic vote in his reelection bid.

"Republicans must find a way to support secure borders, a guest-worker program and comprehensive immigration reform that strengthens citizenship, grows our economy and keeps America a welcoming nation. An anti-Hispanic attitude is suicidal," he concluded.[17]

Rove isn't alone. Syndicated columnist Linda Chavez wrote in the *San Diego Union-Tribune*, "Republicans are finally worried that their failure to attract Hispanic voters in this year's election spells trouble—perhaps for decades. But they're not sure what to do about it. The first thing Republicans have to overcome is a growing belief among Hispanics that they aren't welcome in the party—or in America, for that matter."[18]

It's important to remember that today's undocumented immigrants will be tomorrow's voters. And this consideration ought to be a part of both parties' political calculations. These immigrants represent literally millions of votes.

Being anti-immigration is essentially taking a stance against the future.

The growing political influence of the Latino community is vital to achieving major immigration reform.
There are very few Latinos in the halls of Congress; in
2008, there were only twenty-five Hispanic representatives and three Hispanic senators. No, the Latino community's strength lies in the fact that they have enough votes
to decide the outcome of close elections and that—in less
than one hundred years—there will be more Latinos than
any other ethnic group here in the United States.

It's the Latino wave.

Six

A MANIFESTO FOR A NEW UNITED STATES OF AMERICA

These are new days. What Barack Obama called "the urgency of now"[1] also impels us to look for other changes. Now.

Latinos are the future of the United States, but many changes must be made if they are to become a majority before the end of the century.

It's not just a matter of legalizing undocumented immigrants; it's also essential to protect all minorities. It may appear that the election of Barack Obama signifies that racial prejudice has been completely eliminated from the United States. But the fact that an African American has risen to the highest office in the land does not in itself mean that racism against all minorities in the United States has been completely overcome.

Despite Obama's election, racial prejudice still exists in the United States.

In fact, after his victory, a number of press reports

surfaced about a significant increase in the number of threats and attacks against minorities.

According to the Southern Poverty Law Center, "Hundreds of incidents of abuse or intimidation apparently motivated by racial hatred have been reported since the November 4 election, though most have not involved violence. . . . White supremacist groups such as the Ku Klux Klan and the Council of Conservative Citizens have seen a flood of interest from possible new members since the landmark election of the first black president in U.S. history. Far right groups are also capitalizing on the rising unemployment in the economic downturn and a demographic shift that could make whites a minority by mid-century."[2]

Many of these attacks were directed against Latinos.

But this is nothing new.

Between 2003 and 2007, the number of attacks against Hispanics, just for being Hispanic, increased by 40 percent. And in 2007, Hispanics were the victims of nearly two-thirds of all crimes motivated by ethnicity or national origin.[3]

Every time the United States experiences a crisis—be it economic or security-related—we see an increase in the number of minorities being blamed and attacked. It happened after September 11, and it's happening again during the current financial, housing, and job crisis.

The cycle may be predictable, but that doesn't mean we should tolerate it.

Now that the United States is facing the worst economic crisis since 1929, attacks based on ethnicity or national origin are on the rise again. "In the middle of a recession we can expect economic insecurities to rise and the loss of jobs to result in scapegoating of immigrants," said Milton Rosado, president of the Labor Council for Latin American Advancement, or LCLAA. "This is a dangerous combination that can lead to an increase in the number of hate crimes against Latinos."[4]

Consider these two horrible examples.

In November of 2008, Marcelo Lucero, a thirty-seven-year old Ecuadorean immigrant, was attacked and stabbed to death by seven young white men from Patchogue, Long Island, New York. All the suspects were apprehended shortly after the attack. According to the Suffolk County Police Department, the defendants "simply wanted to beat up someone who looked Hispanic."[5]

Local police from across the nation reported to the FBI that there were a total of 830 victims of anti-Hispanic crimes in 595 incidents in 2007.[6] These numbers represent increases over previous years, based on the annual reports mandated by the Hate Crime Statistics Act.

Another case. One month after Lucero's murder, an Ecuadorean man by the name of José Sucuzhañay was leaving a Brooklyn bar with his brother, Romel, when they were attacked by three young men armed with baseball bats and shouting anti-Hispanic and anti-homosexual slurs. José died in the hospital two days after the attack, and one day before his mother arrived from Ecuador.[7]

Despite Obama's triumph, racism continues to be the

primary social problem in the United States. It can no longer stop an African American from becoming president, but it still has an effect.

A 2007 survey done by Sergio Bendixen for the Inter-American Development Bank's Multilateral Investment Fund corroborates this view. According to the survey, "A vast majority [of Mexican and Central American immigrants] felt discrimination against Latin Americans has grown."[8]

We must conclude that much remains to be done to overcome the obstacles Hispanic Americans, Latin American immigrants, and those of other ethnicities and nationalities face as they work to become fully integrated into American culture. One man, Barack Obama, cannot instantly reverse the prejudice and backward thinking that have been decades in the making.

Words Matter

This reversal could begin with the language we use. Words matter. The way we speak can either bring us closer together or push us to the edge, and maybe even over the edge.

In recent years, the immigration debate has been charged with hatred and divisiveness. We very rarely see undocumented immigration as a national problem that affects all of us. Nor do we recognize that we all must participate in finding a solution.

Radio talk shows and the Internet are often rife with

offensive, denigrating references to undocumented immigrants. Perhaps these forms of media allow people to hide their faces more than they can on television. We must expose the unjust and destructive effects of this language and work to quell it.

Many anti-immigrant activists speak of undocumented workers as if they shouldn't be treated as fellow human beings who—like it or not—participate in and influence the daily lives of all Americans. And I always have to ask myself if the people on the attack have ever tried to put themselves in an immigrant's shoes.

But what's most glaring is the total lack of dialogue on the issue. There is no discourse. The conversation about immigration is too often nothing more than an exchange of accusations and allegations between those on either side of the issue.

The voices of the undocumented immigrants themselves are vital to this conversation. And those voices are largely absent from the debate. That is part of my motivation for writing this book. I want to lend my voice to those who have yet to be heard. I want to help the invisibles come out into the light.

When was the last time you heard an undocumented immigrant being interviewed on the nightly news?

Their voices, explanations, expectations, and hopes go wholly unheard in English. The voices we do hear, however, come from the people protected by a microphone or a position of power speaking about the costs and disadvantages of immigration. They rarely focus on the valuable contributions and benefits that immigrants bring to our society.

We need to break down these barriers and establish a conversation in which immigration opponents, immigration supporters, and the immigrants themselves can all speak and can all be heard. The solution can exist only within this triangle.

This is not just a question of power; it is also a question of language. The unilateral diatribes, which only generate more hatred and misunderstanding, must be put to rest. We need to sit down with the most extreme radio and television commentators and establish a set of parameters for controlling the debate. And it all begins with using the correct terminology.

First of all, we must abolish the practice of referring to people as *illegals*. They're not. No human being is inherently *illegal*. They are simply people without legal documents permitting them to live in the United States.

It's very encouraging to note that both President Obama and his former opponent Senator McCain avoid use of the word *illegal*. This is an important provision, because it clearly outlines the parameters of the debate and prevents insults and anger from arising.

Before Sonia Sotomayor became a judge on the Supreme Court, the term "illegal immigrant" had been registered in dozens of cases. The *New York Times* found that Judge Sotomayor set an example in 2009 by using the term "undocumented immigrant" for the first time in the case of *Mohawk Industries v. Carpenter*.

Using the term *illegal* implies that we're talking about criminal offenders. That's not the case. The vast majority of undocumented immigrants have committed no criminal acts or serious offenses beyond their lack of documentation.

It's not fair to hold undocumented immigrants criminally responsible while at the same time benefiting from their work. And every single one of us living in the United States does benefit from their labor.

Yes, undocumented immigrants violated the law, but millions of American citizens and thousands of American companies are complicit in this violation by hiring them to avoid complying with minimum wage and safety regulations. These individuals and corporations are not referred to as *illegal*.

For all these reasons, selecting and using the proper terminology is fundamental for changing the tone of this debate. It allows us to begin by giving the undocumented immigrants their sense of humanity back. It reminds us to treat them as people who—just like the rest of us—live and work here in the United States. They have the same concerns about their families, their health care, and their jobs. The difference—the only difference—is on paper. That's all.

Ultimately, it comes down to a very simple concept: providing a piece of paper that legalizes the status of undocumented workers in the United States.

How hard would it really be to erase the first two letters from the word *illegal* or the first two letters of the word *undocumented?*

Three Essential Elements

There are three elements that are essential for comprehensive immigration reform: legalization, integration, and long-term investment.

As with other complicated social issues, periodic adjustments must be made to existing immigration policy so that the laws keep pace with the reality of the world in which we live. But because of the enormous complexity of the immigration phenomenon in the United States, the rules of the game are often slow to change.

We are long overdue. The last adjustment made to U.S. immigration policy was the Immigration Reform and Control Act of 1986. Before that action there was a twenty-one-year gap, dating back to the reforms made in 1965. From then you have to go back thirty-six more years—to the Registry Act of 1929—to find another case of immigration laws being changed.

The U.S. immigration system does not work, and immediate attention is required if we hope to respond adequately to the demands of the twenty-first century. You have only to look at the incredible delays and waiting periods—often more than a decade—that elapse before a family can be reunited or resolve an immigration conflict. This is totally unacceptable. In fact, it's Kafkaesque. Profound, fundamental reform is urgently needed.

More than two decades have gone by since the last modifications were made to an inefficient, antiquated policy that urgently needs renovation if it is going to adapt to meet the nation's changing requirements.

But it would be a grave mistake to think that simply increasing enforcement—with more agents and more fencing along the border, and more workplace raids and deportations—will solve what is primarily an economic problem. For reforms to succeed, everything needs to be put in place in the proper order. If we implement coercive methods first, nothing substantive will be achieved.

The first priority must be to address the undocumented immigrants already living in the United States, and those who arrive here each and every day. Then, through the use of new technology, we can create a more organized and efficient method of controlling the border at ports of entry, companies, and offices. Finally, we must invest in Latin America so workers can find well-paying jobs in their own countries instead of having to migrate north for opportunities.

So what, exactly, would a comprehensive immigration bill require? There are three essential elements.

1. Legalization

Legalizing undocumented workers already living in the United States is a vital component of any new immigration law. It is impossible to talk about immigration reform without legalization.

The main purpose, both inside and outside of Congress, of reforming immigration policy has always been to provide decent living and working conditions for the millions

who live in fear of persecution and deportation from the
United States. This is a country that promises equality for
all. The Bill of Rights doesn't say that only American
citizens should be protected. Everyone, including undocumented immigrants, should be treated fairly. It is our moral
obligation to find a way to fully integrate these immigrants
into American society and ensure that they are subject
to and receive all the protections of this nation's laws.

How can this be accomplished? Even though there is an
increasing consensus on the fact that something must be
done about legalizing undocumented immigrants, there is
little agreement about how to do it.

This is not to say that undocumented immigrants should
have an unfair advantage over those who have waited
patiently for years, following all the requirements to
become permanent legal residents of the United States.

Any reform should include a monetary penalty for
undocumented immigrants. A fine will show that there are
negative consequences for those who enter or stay in the
country illegally, while at the same time allowing an
opportunity for undocumented immigrants to make
amends and move forward. The process of admitting fault
and paying a price ensures that this immigration reform is
not criticized as being a form of amnesty, and the funds
collected could be used to offset a large portion of the
budgetary expense involved in legalizing workers.

Amnesty implies a pardon. Amnesty implies receiving
a benefit without having to give anything in return. It is
important to understand that these undocumented immi-

grants *are* willing to give something in return for their legalization.

The total integration of those already living in the United States must be an objective of any immigration reform. This is fundamental. It is not enough for undocumented immigrants to hope only for work permits, temporary or permanent, or eventual legal residency. We must give undocumented workers a path to citizenship, even if it takes many years. This is the great promise—and the great gift—that the United States has historically made.

We cannot have first-class and second-class workers. We must achieve the complete integration of American society.

Inevitably, the current economic situation makes the promotion and advancement of any immigration reform more difficult. In this climate of crisis we are living through, immigration reform must also take into account the protection of jobs for American-born citizens. If Americans feel that undocumented workers are a threat to their own employment, it will be extremely difficult to find any political support in Washington for making the necessary changes.

Far from taking jobs from Americans, undocumented immigrants create employment and complement their labor. One needs only to observe operations in a restaurant, a hotel, or even an orchard to see that most immigrants are working in kitchens, doing housekeeping, or picking fruit and vegetables; they are not taking the chef's, the manager's, or the owner's job. Undocumented immigrants are primarily employed in the support positions that make it possible for these businesses to run smoothly. Even with the rising unemployment we are currently facing, few Americans have been competing for these jobs.

It is important to remember that these workers are also consumers. The immediate and massive retreat of millions of customers would ruin thousands of businesses in the United States. Rather than being a threat to economic growth, undocumented immigrants make growth possible. If they are fully integrated into the economic system, the benefits will multiply in the form of larger tax payments and an increase in consumption.

Finally, this issue is time sensitive: the longer it takes us to solve this problem, the worse it gets. We can't put off finding a solution any longer. Even with the economic problems we are facing, more undocumented immigrants arrive in the United States every day. We cannot forget that the economic crisis in Latin America began later than in the United States and, therefore, will take longer to resolve itself. In addition, Latin American economies can't adjust to changes in the world's markets as rapidly as our economy.

As soon as the recession begins to ease and U.S. businesses start hiring again, we will be facing a new wave of Latin American immigrants. If our immigration policies have not been reformed we won't be ready for this new wave.

2. Integration

The United States needs a system that effectively integrates the hundreds of thousands of immigrants who come here every year.

It would be disingenuous to take the position that reform will prevent undocumented immigration. Whether it's in greater or lesser numbers, people will continue to come into the United States illegally. We have to be very realistic and look at the situation objectively in order to make an effective plan.

It could take decades to see wage equity between the United States and Latin America. And it's even possible that we won't see that in our lifetime. This means that millions of people will continue to emigrate from the poor nations to those that are wealthy. We have only to look at Mexico, which is not only facing a decline in its economic growth and foreign investment, and an increase in unemployment and crime (due to the increasing power of Mexico's drug cartels), but is seeing one of its main sources of income—tourism—suffer due to the H1N1 flu epidemic. When Mexican families consider where they would have a better life, many decide not to wait any longer for the promised changes, and decide they'd rather live in a country that has already been built rather than wait in a country that is under construction.

Several studies have suggested that at least half a million undocumented immigrants enter the United States every year. This number has shrunk drastically as a result of our economic crisis, but it is a temporary reduction.

This decrease confirms what is often stated by economists: that undocumented immigrants are attracted to the United States by the promise of jobs. If there are no jobs, they don't come. Sooner or later the economy will recover and the number of immigrants will go up again. The United States needs to be ready to receive millions of immigrants in the next few years. And currently it isn't.

The immigration amnesty of 1986 failed, among other reasons, because it didn't provide an effective mechanism for integrating new immigrants into the country. We must not make the same mistake again. It is vital that any immigration reform address not only those undocumented immigrants currently in the United States but also the hundreds of thousands of immigrants who will continue to arrive in the future. Without an ongoing plan we will have to deal with new reforms in less than a decade.

This needs to be done now. And it needs to be done well.

A system of quotas would not work because it would be imposed by a bureaucracy or by Congress and most likely would not adapt quickly and effectively to the fluctuations of the job market. But opening up the border and letting employment supply and demand determine the number of immigrants who enter the country isn't realistic or desirable either. Then what?

We need a program that is flexible, that can respond quickly, that can mesh immigrants looking for work with jobs that are available in the country. Earlier, for example, we were talking about half a million a year. At the beginning of 2009 that number went down to about a quarter million. And in the future, no doubt, it will go up. The program requires quick adjustments and independence from the complicated and slow-moving political and bureaucratic procedures in Washington.

This employment program is fundamental if we want to regain control of the border. In order for it to work, it has to be easier and more attractive for immigrants to follow this employment program than to risk their lives crossing deserts, mountains, and rivers.

If the United States creates a successful program, the border with Mexico will be easier to handle and Border Patrol will be able to go after real, dangerous criminals. Control of the border is achievable not with the use of force, but with a system that has the capacity to integrate the hundreds of thousands of immigrants who enter the United States every year.

The question remains: Once this employment program is in place, what do we do with those immigrants who were able to enter the United States legally? How long will they be allowed to stay?

These questions are central to the debate on immigration, and Congress will have the final say. Initially, there should be a program for temporary workers doing cyclical jobs such as agriculture. Those workers could be in the United States with a work permit during a specific time frame.

However, it's not enough to create a program only for temporary workers. We need another program that takes into consideration the fact that the vast majority of immigrants entering the United States do not return to their country of origin, but remain here in permanent jobs.

They don't intentionally deceive the U.S. government or lie on their entry applications. The reality is that as soon as immigrants get jobs that offer ten or twenty times more than the ones they left behind, they think of staying. As soon as immigrants have American children, they think of staying. As soon as immigrants improve their lifestyle and opportunities for the future, they think of staying. This is the magic that the United States holds for those who arrive, and it would be unrealistic not to take that into consideration.

It is very important to stress that this doesn't signify a mass invasion of foreigners, nor does it alter the essence of the United States. Many countries, such as Australia, have a much higher percentage of foreigners than the United States—and if we make a quick historical analysis we will see the United States had a higher percentage of immigrants during the twentieth century than it does now.

If we want the next immigration reform to be successful and we want to prevent having to change it every decade, then we must face the problem proactively and see immigration as a source of growth and prosperity for the United States. This requires at least two things: First, considerably increasing the number of legal immigrants that are allowed into this country each year. And second, establishing a new path for immigrants, sooner or later, to become U.S. citizens.

This—not the use of force—is what will give the United States real control over its border.

3. Long-term Investment

We must create a long-term plan for creating incentives (like high-paying jobs and educational opportunities) in developing countries so that people don't need to leave their homeland in order to sustain themselves and their families.

It is tragic that Latin America's main export is its strongest, most visionary and ambitious youth. Unfortunately this is not going to change until they find good jobs and opportunities for growth in the places they were born.

The United States must reestablish communication and close cooperation with countries in Latin America. Those bonds were significantly weakened after the terrorist attacks of September 11, 2001, during George W. Bush's presidency. Although none of the nineteen terrorists were Latin American and no country in Latin America was involved in the attacks against the United States, the consequences in the region were profoundly negative.

The rapprochement between the United States and the Latin American region must address the issue of commerce. But that isn't enough. New technology demands more cooperation on issues that appeared to be exclusive to each country in the past, such as education and health. The exchange of technology, educational methods, and medical advances will generate new fields of development in Latin America.

In addition, we haven't made the most of the thousands of Latin American communities within the United States. The members of these communities retain ties to their homelands; if they are properly organized, they can participate in investment and development programs in the cities they left behind. This will be so much more helpful than simply sending financial aid.

As Vice President Joe Biden stated during his first trip to Central America in 2009, right now the U.S. can't afford to make a large investment in Latin American countries. However, we have a viable alternative if we approach investing on a much smaller scale.

Above and beyond cooperation among governments, we must encourage communication between similar communities on both sides of the border. I know many Mexicans, Colombians, and Salvadorans, just to mention three nationalities, in the United States who would be eager to invest in projects in their countries of origin, such as schools, sports centers, parks, or environmental programs—if they were guaranteed that their money wouldn't end up in the hands of corrupt politicians.

It would be so easy for a Mexican family in Los Angeles to sponsor the education of one or two children in Michoacán through the end of high school. Or for an Ecuadorean family in New York to buy a computer for a classroom in Guayaquil. Or for a Colombian family in Miami to enable the vaccination of ten children in Barranquilla. Or for a Honduran family in Houston to collaborate in the purchase of sewing machines for a small business in Tegucigalpa. All these things will be possible if we establish informal bridges of communication between Latin American communities in the United States and those in their country of origin.

This collaboration would require Latin American governments to identify those projects that are a priority and enlist, through their consulates, the participation and

investment of communities in the United States. It is complicated, but it can be done. It certainly beats relying on a
government megaproject, which often means resigning
oneself to a permanent wait.

In the long run, both government and private efforts
would help reduce undocumented immigration by promoting education, health, and creation of jobs in Latin
America. Currently there is no infrastructure to implement such programs. Now is the time for our governments
to act as facilitators for this sort of investment.

In order to regain control of our borders we must create a system for legalizing Latin American immigrants
who already live in the United States and fully integrating
future immigrants, as well as promoting long-term investment among communities with as little interference as
possible from bureaucracies.

The White House seems to be aware of the pressing need
to attack the United States' immigration problem on a
multitude of fronts, and its Web site includes the following
elements in a possible solution:

"For too long, politicians in Washington have exploited
the immigration issue to divide the nation rather than find
real solutions. Our broken immigration system can only
be fixed by putting politics aside and offering a complete
solution that secures our border, enforces our laws, and
reaffirms our heritage as a nation of immigrants.

"Create Secure Borders: Protect the integrity of our borders. Support additional personnel, infrastructure and technology on the border and at our ports of entry.

"Improve Our Immigration System: Fix the dysfunctional immigration bureaucracy and increase the number of legal immigrants to keep families together and meet the demand for jobs that employers cannot fill.

"Remove Incentives to Enter Without Documents: Remove incentives to enter the country by cracking down on employers who hire undocumented immigrants.

"Bring People Out of the Shadows: Support a system that allows undocumented immigrants who are in good standing to pay a fine, learn English, and go to the back of the line for the opportunity to become citizens.

"Work with Mexico: Promote economic development in Mexico to decrease undocumented immigration."[9]

It's important to recognize that there are a number of possible solutions to the immigration problem. And we must avoid resorting to the initial impulses of those extreme groups who call for more fencing, more raids, and more Border Patrol agents. That is not the solution. If these three measures—legalization, integration, and long-term investment—are put into practice, even partially, the United States would be able to regain control of its borders and workplaces. An excellent way to measure whether new reforms are working will be a reduction in the use of force when dealing with immigration issues.

In addition to being a social and economic issue, immigration is a political one. Without a doubt, President Obama and the Democratic Party know that passing immigration reform would translate into more Latino votes in the future and that Latinos are an increasingly influential minority group. But reform won't pass without Republican support, and it is essential that we include the GOP in the debate and in the decision-making process.

For example, it would be very difficult for immigration reform to pass in Congress without the support of Senator John McCain. But the few Republicans who so far have favored reform have to convince their party colleagues that these changes are urgent, economically productive, and in line with America's principles—and thus something that should ultimately find support in both parties. A negative vote on immigration reform would put the GOP at odds, again, with the fastest-growing bloc in the American electorate: the Hispanic voter.

Successfully reforming U.S. immigration policy requires a pragmatic vision, not a political or ideological one. And that's precisely the challenge: to separate ourselves from the clamor of extremists and identify a solution that corresponds to the guiding principle of the Declaration of Independence—that all men are created equal.

AFTERWORD

My Twenty-five Years in the United States

In 1980, not long before I came to live in Los Angeles, the Census Bureau estimated that only 15 million Latinos were living in the United States. In the twenty-five years that I've been here, that number has tripled.

I just happened to be on the cusp of the Latino wave.

And that's why I'm convinced that eventually the United States will treat its millions of undocumented immigrants with the same generosity that it has showed me for the past quarter of a century.

The United States is a place of improbable stories, of lives that never could have been realized anywhere else in the world. I don't believe that my life as a journalist, free to write what I please, and all the possibilities that grew from it would have been possible in any other country. That's why I came here to live.

The United States offered me opportunities that Mexico could not.

My past is written. It's immutable. There is no way to change it, even if I wanted to. When I was growing up, I never even imagined that one day I would be an immigrant. But later in my life it became a necessity. If I wanted the freedom to be a journalist and to cover news around the world, I had no choice but to leave Mexico for the United States.

The United States has allowed me to shape my own future.

Not many countries offer second chances. The United States gave me that, and it continues to give second chances to many, many others.

The United States is both the country that magnanimously adopted me and the country that I chose as my adoptive home.

You can't select the country where you're born. But a lucky few can choose the country in which they live. The United States has been giving that opportunity to millions of immigrants for well over two centuries now.

The United States of America is still a young nation (at least when compared with the majority of other nations around the globe), yet it has matured profoundly in terms of understanding the importance of diversity, tolerance, and openness when it comes to accepting those who come from afar. It's a country that has grown up quickly.

The United States has rapidly become the country of the future—the country of all our futures—with the Founding Fathers' understanding that its strength lay in the defense of our differences. And what separates the

United States from other nations is that here, our prospects for the future tend to be better than those present and those past. That's the promise.

Today the United States is my home, and the home of my children. It's the place where I found the belief that they—Paola and Nicolás—will have better lives than I had. And I continue to believe that.

The United States is the place where a foreigner can reinvent himself, and suddenly find millions of others like him.

Ultimately, this is the place where foreigners cease to be foreign.

After twenty-five years in this country, I have the utmost confidence that the United States will eventually do the right thing when it comes to immigration reform, the fight against racism, and the defense of human rights.

This is a country that works to correct its errors, that refuses to become mired in the past, and that pushes ever onward into the future. I find it fascinating that immigrants often have as much or more confidence in the system and the opportunities it offers than many native-born American citizens. I'm not alone in that.

Clearly, the United States is undergoing a process of Latinization. With the enormous growth in the Hispanic population comes the growing influence wielded by Hispanics in American culture and society.

But, at the same time, it's important to promote the Americanization of the new Hispanics and Latin American immigrants who live here. And this is where the theme of legalization comes into play. It would be a grave mistake to neglect revising current immigration policy to more effectively integrate the millions of people whose greatest dream is to become part of these United States.

If we want all immigrants to speak English, learn American customs, and otherwise assimilate into American society, we must provide them with the ability to come out of the shadows legally, become visible, and live here without fear. Legalization is simply a way of Americanizing undocumented workers.

As I said at the beginning of this book, the greatest nations are defined by how they treat their weakest inhabitants and by the way they integrate them into society at large.

Rescuing the most vulnerable people—the undocumented immigrants, the invisibles—and truly making them a part of this nation has been a point of pride for the United States throughout its history. We're not asking for anything new.

A quarter of a century ago, I came to the country where the Declaration of Independence assured us that we are all created equal. And now is the time to keep this promise alive. We are simply asking this country to honor its history and its name. We are asking the United States to be the *United* States.

Nothing more. Nothing less.

ACKNOWLEDGMENTS

To Milena Alberti, Jeff Alexander, Lisa Weinert, and the entire team at Vintage/Random House for adopting me, believing in this project, and seeing the grand vision of a multiethnic, multilingual, and multicultural United States.

To my agent and friend René Alegría, who once again strikes out on this adventure with me, only this time without a parachute.

To my colleagues at Univision, who support me every single day, and with whom I share the great pleasure of chasing down the news and doing what I love to do the most.

To those great Latino pioneers Cesar Chavez, Dolores Huerta, Julian Samora, Raul Yzaguirre, and Henry Cisneros, who have carved out the path for the rest of us. The present and the future of the United States could not be understood without you.

To my children, Paola and Nicolás, because—in the end—everything I do is for you. Thanks to you, I am able to see this country through your eyes.

To Ana, who has filled me with book titles, hopes, and life.

NOTES

One: The Invisibles

[1] Jeffrey Passel, "Trends in Unauthorized Immigration: Undocumented Inflow Now Trails Legal Inflow," Pew Hispanic Center, October 2, 2008.

[2] Ibid. Estimated U.S. unauthorized immigration population by region and country of birth, 2008. Based on March supplements to the current population survey.

[3] Spencer S. Hsu, "Cleaning Firm Used Illegal Workers at Chertoff Home," *Washington Post*, December 11, 2008.

[4] Ibid.

[5] Remarks by former homeland security secretary Michael Chertoff at the 2008 End-of-the-Year Address, Department of Homeland Security, December 18, 2008.

[6] *ABC World News*, George W. Bush, interview by Charles Gibson, December 2, 2008.

[7] Alfonso Chardy, "U.S. Steps Up Deportation of Illegal Immigrants," *Miami Herald*, December 10, 2008. "From Sept. 30, 2007 to Oct. 1 of this year, at least 349,041 foreign nationals were deported—a 20 percent increase over the previous 12-month period." According to the Border Patrol, 723,825 undocumented immigrants were arrested in 2008: 661,766 were Mexican and 62,059 from other countries; 19,346 were from Honduras, 16,396 from Guatemala, 12,068 from El Salvador, and 1,466 from Nicaragua (CBP 2008

fiscal year in review, http://www.cbp.gov/xp/cgov/newsroom/highlights/08year_review.xml).

[8] ICE, Fiscal Year 2007 Annual Report. In 2007, 276,912 were deported.

[9] Jennifer Ludden, "Immigration Experts Predict Fewer Workplace Raids," *All Things Considered*, NPR, December 2, 2008, www.npr.org.

[10] Ibid.

[11] "Hypocrisy on Immigration," *Washington Post* editorial, March 17, 2007, http://www.washingtonpost.com/wp-dyn/content/article/2007/03/16/AR2007031602119.html.

[12] Migration Policy Institute. "Collateral Damage: An Examination of ICE's Fugitive Operations Program," February 4, 2009.

[13] Jorge Ramos, "Obama, Latinos, and Latin America," Univision.com, June 2, 2008, http://www.univision.com/content/content.jhtml?cid=1553033.

[14] Julia Preston, "Immigration Quandary: A Mother Torn from Her Baby," *New York Times*, November 17, 2007.

[15] Lamar Smith, letter to the editor, *New York Times*, August 26, 2008. Smith, a Republican from Texas, is the ranking member of the House Judiciary Committee.

[16] Immigration Policy Center, "A comprehensive guide to immigration," August 3, 2009.

[17] Jorge Ramos, "Obama, Latinos, and Latin America."

[18] Jorge Ramos, "Face-to-face with McCain: Exclusive Interview by Jorge Ramos," Univision.com, September 18, 2008, http://www.univision.com/content/content.jhtml?cid=1669229.

Two: A Nation of Equals

[1] Universal Declaration of Human Rights, United Nations, December 10, 1948.

[2] Alexis de Tocqueville, *Democracy in America* (Cambridge: Cambridge University Press, 1863).

[3] Abraham Lincoln, Peoria speech, October 1854, *The Collected Works of Abraham Lincoln*, ed. Roy P. Basler, *American Historical Review* (1953), 247.

[4] Martin Luther King. "I have a dream," speech, August 28, 1963, *A Testament of Hope: The Essential Writings and Speeches of Martin Luther King* (New York: HarperOne, 1990), 217.

[5] Immigration Policy Center, "De-Romanticizing Our Immigrant Past: Why Claiming 'My Family Came Legally' Is Often a Myth," November 25, 2008.

[6] Immigration Policy Center, "Opportunity and Exclusion: A Brief History of U.S. Immigration Policy," November 25, 2008.

[7] Peter S. Canellos, "Obama Victory Took Root in Kennedy-inspired Immigration Act," *Boston Globe*, November 11, 2008. "[The 1965 Immigration Act] transformed a nation 85 percent white in 1965 into one that's one-third minority today, and on track for a nonwhite majority by 2042. . . . In the 1950s, 53 percent of all immigrants were Europeans and just 6 percent were Asians; by the 1990s, just 16 percent were Europeans and 31 percent were Asians. The percentages of Latino and African immigrants also jumped significantly."

[8] Oprah Winfrey, *The Oprah Winfrey Show*, CBS, December 16, 2008.

Three: Ten Reasons for Immigration Reform

[1] Maribel Hastings, "Economic Arguments for Legalization," America's Voice, March 25, 2009.

[2] Reuters, "Illegal Imigrants Not U.S. Health Care Burden," November 26, 2007.

[3] Immigration Policy Center, *From Anecdotes to Evidence: Setting the Record Straight on Immigrants and Crime*, September 10, 2008, http://www.immigrationpolicy.org/images/File/factcheck/SettingtheRecordStraightonImmigrantsandCrime9-10-08.pdf.

[4] Richard Nadles, "Immigration and the Wealth of States," Americas Majority Foundation, January 2008, p. 9. Included in ibid.

[5] Cnn.com, "Minorities Expected to Be Majority in 2050," August 13, 2008, http://www.cnn.com/2008/US/08/13/census.minorities/index.html. "By 2050, the 65-and-older age group will increase to 88.5 million, more than doubling its current number of 38.7 million."

[6] Richard Fry, "Latinos in Higher Education: Many Enroll, Too Few Graduate," Pew Hispanic Center, September 5, 2002.

[7] Alan Greenspan, statement before the Special Committee on Aging, United States Senate, February 27, 2003.

[8] Laura Parker, "USA Just Wouldn't Work Without Immigrant Labor," *USA Today*, July 22, 2001.

[9] Ben Bernanke, testimony before the House Budget Committee, February 28, 2007.

[10] Homeland Security, Office of Immigration Service, "U.S. Legal Permanent Residents: 2007."

[11] National Immigration Forum Report (Autumn 1994). "Six out of ten" enter the United States with a tourist, business, or student visa and eventually violate the terms of that visa.

[12] Department of Homeland Security press release, December 18, 2008.

[13] Jonathan Weisman, "With Senate Vote, Congress Passes Border Fence Bill," *Washington Post*, September 30, 2006.

[14] "CBP Meets 18,000 Border Patrol Agent Hiring Commitment Weeks Early," December 17, 2008, http://www.cbp.gov/xp/cgov/newsroom/news_releases/archives/2008_news_releases/december_2008/12172008_9.xml.

[15] Rebeca Logan, "Vigilancia fronteriza tiene cara latina," BBC World News, January 1, 2009.

[16] "CBP Meets 18,000."

[17] National Council of La Raza, "Dream Act," www.nclr.org/content/policy/detail/1331/.

[18] Jesse Bogan, Kerry A. Dolan, Christopher Helman, and Nathan Vardi, "The Next Disaster: Narco Violence Is Exploding—Just as Oil Prices Are Plunging and Mexico Is Bracing for a Deep U.S. Recession," *Forbes*, December 22, 2008.

[19] National Human Rights Commission (Mexico) report, *Univision News*, December 16, 2008.

[20] Bogan, et al., "The Next Disaster."

[21] Associated Press, "Mexico's Banamex: Remittances May Drop More," January 13, 2009.

[22] Associated Press, "Remittances Increase from Salvadorans in the U.S.," October 17, 2008.

[23] "Inmigrantes guatemaltecos enviaron USD 1.756 millones," ACAN-EFE, June 12, 2008.

[24] *Newsweek*/MSNBC/www.fallenheroesmemorial.com.

[25] Jorge Ramos, "Obama, Latinos, and Latin America."

[26] Barack Obama, statement on U.S. Senate floor, May 23, 2007, www.whitehouse.gov.

[27] Jorge Ramos, "Face-to-face with McCain."

[28] Gannett News Service,"Reid Says Democrats to Tackle Big Issues," November 23, 2008.

[29] Harry Reid, interview by Jorge Ramos, *Al Punto*, Univision, January 18, 2009.

[30] Immigration Policy Center, "De-Romanticizing Our Immigrant Past.

Four: The First Hispanic President of the United States

[1] Sam Roberts, "In a Generation, Minorities May Be the U.S. Majority," *New York Times*, August 14, 2008.

[2] This is the result of a number of calculations. The Census Bureau estimates that the Hispanic population will grow from 15 percent in 2008 to 30 percent in 2050. In other words, it will go from 47 million people in 2008 to 133 million in forty-two years. This implies a .357 percent annual increase. Using those figures, and assuming that Hispanics will swell to 30 percent of the population in forty-two years, another fifty-six years will need to elapse for them to reach 50 percent of the total U.S. population. Therefore, I arrived at the year 2106, when a projected 221 million Hispanics will be living in the U.S., representing over half of the country's population.

[3] Sam Roberts, "In a Generation, Minorities May Be the U.S. Majority."

[4] Associated Press, "Nearly 12 Million Mexicans Said to Reside in the U.S.," August 20, 2008. "Mexico says 11.8 million of its citizens now live in the United States . . . and 21.5 percent of those have U.S. citizenship. Immigration official Ana Teresa Aranda says some 580,000 Mexican nationals emigrate each year."

[5] Sam Roberts, "In a Generation, Minorities May Be the U.S. Majority."

[6] Richard Fry, "Latino Settlement in the New Century," Pew Hispanic Center, October 23, 2008.

[7] Robert Bernstein, "U.S. Hispanic Population Surpasses 45 Million, Now 15 Percent of Total," U.S. Census Bureau, May 1, 2008.

[8] Kat Glass/MCT, "Los Hispanos Salvan a Estados Unidos de la Crisis Demográfica," *El Nuevo Herald*, August 19, 2008.

[9] U.S. Census Bureau, May 1, 2008.

[10] Katrin Bennhold, "Rapper With Attitude Updates 'Frenchness,'" *International Herald Tribune*, June 6, 2007.

[11] Henry Cisneros, *Latinos and the Nation's Future* (Houston: Arte Público Press, 2008).

[12] John Leguizamo, interview, CNN Entertainment, 1998.

[13] Michael Powell, "The Caucus: Native Tongues and More," *New York Times*, July 12, 2008.

[14] Ibid.

[15] Andrés Oppenheimer, "Obama y la enseñanza del español," *El Nuevo Herald*, July 17, 2008.

[16] "Obama Tells Audience, 'You Need to Make Sure Your Child Can Speak Spanish," *Business Wire*, July 9, 2008.

[17] *Good Morning America*, ABC News Internet Ventures, October 8, 2007. Analysis by Peyton M. Craighill.

[18] Mauro Mujica, interview by Jaime García, *Univision News*, July 10, 2008.

[19] "Obama Tells Audience."

[20] Republican Party platform for the National Convention, Minneapolis, September 1–4, 2008.

[21] José Vasconcelos, *The Cosmic Race* (Baltimore: Johns Hopkins University Press, 1997).

[22] Robert Bernstein, "U.S. Hispanic Population."

Five: The Latino Vote 2008

[1] National Association of Latino Elected and Appointed Officials (NALEO) Survey, November 20, 2008.

[2] U.S. Census Bureau, "U.S. Voter Turnout Up in 2004, Census Bureau Reports," May 26, 2005.

[3] NALEO Survey, November 20, 2008.

[4] Pew Hispanic Center analysis of 2008 exit poll results, as reported by CNN.

[5] "Bush's Final Approval Rating: 22 Percent," *CBS Evening News*, January 16, 2009.

[6] Mark Hugo Lopez, "How Hispanics Voted in the 2008 Election," Pew Research Center, November 5, 2008.

[7] Paul Taylor and Richard Fry, "Hispanics and the 2008 Election: A Swing Vote?" Pew Hispanic Center, December 6, 2007.

[8] Robert de Posada, "Republicans Rapidly Losing Ground Among Hispanic Voters," The Latino Coalition, January 5, 2006.

[9] Damien Cave, "Democrats See Cuba Travel Limits as Campaign Issue in Florida," *New York Times*, June 1, 2008.

[10] NALEO Survey, November 20, 2008.

[11] José Cancela, *The Power of Business en Español* (New York: Rayo/HarperCollins, 2007).

[12] Sam Roberts, "In U.S. Name Count, Garcias Are Catching Up with Joneses," *New York Times*, November 17, 2007.

[13] CNN-Univision Democratic Presidential Debate, University of Texas–Austin, February 21, 2008.

[14] Ibid.

[15] "More Immigration Losers," *Wall Street Journal*, December 2, 2008.

[16] Mitch McConnell, speech, Republican National Committee winter meeting, January 29, 2009.

[17] Karl Rove, "A Way Out of the Wilderness," *Newsweek*, November 15, 2008.

[18] Linda Chavez, "How to Get Hispanics into the GOP," *San Diego Union-Tribune*, November 22, 2008.

Six: A Manifesto for a New United States of America

[1] Barack Obama, speech in Dallas, Texas, February 20, 2008.

[2] Mathew Bigg, "Election of Obama Provokes Rise in U.S. Hate Crimes," Reuters, November 24, 2008.

[3] "LCLAA and Global Exchange Concerned with Growing Anti-Immigrant/Latino Attacks," November 21, 2007. Hate Crimes Statistics released by the Federal Bureau of Investigation and reported by the Labor Council for Latin American Advancement (LCLAA).

[4] Milton Rosado, ibid.

[5] Deepti Hajela and Frank Eltman, "Advocates Say Rhetoric Fuels Anti-Hispanic Crime," Associated Press, November 12, 2008.

[6] Ibid.

[7] Kareem Fahim and Karen Zraick, "A Death Shakes Up Ecuadoreans as They Make Their Mark in New York," *New York Times*, December 15, 2008.

[8] Inter-American Development Bank, "Survey Finds Lower Percentage of Mexican Migrants Sending Money Home from the United States," news release, August 8, 2007, http://www.iadb.org/news/detail.cfm?artid=3985&language=En&id=3985&CFID=316254&CFTOKEN=99927738.

[9] "Immigration," The White House, http://www.whitehouse.gov/agenda/immigration.

Meet with Interesting People
Enjoy Stimulating Conversation
Discover Wonderful Books